How To Write News For Broadcast And Print Media

To

Cathy

Carol

Cindy

Cris

No. 643
$9.95

How To Write News For Broadcast And Print Media

By David Dary

TAB BOOKS
Blue Ridge Summit, Pa. 17214

Preface

Since this book attracted your attention, you probably are interested in news writing. Good! News writing is a fascinating and challenging profession, whether you choose print or broadcast news.

If you are a beginner interested in learning how to write news, this book will aim you in the right direction. But it alone will not teach you to write. No book will. News writing must be learned by writing, and you, as an aspiring journalist, must be prepared for much hard work. Good news writing—any good writing—is the result of much thought and effort.

On the pages that follow, you will find a thumbnail sketch of journalism's history—the foundation on which the profession is based. Then we examine what news is and how it is gathered. The balance of the book is devoted to the basic techniques of news writing and the application of those principles to print and broadcast, plus a chapter dealing with feature stories and a chapter summarizing the important laws and regulations that affect the news writer.

Whether professional journalists will find anything of value within these covers will depend upon their background and experience. For the newspaper journalist, this book may provide a better understanding of broadcast news writing, and vice versa.

Although this effort is a simple and basic primer for beginning news writers, it may help every journalist realize that there is very little difference in good news writing, whether for print or broadcast. Actually, the major difference is in the manner of delivery and presentation.

I want to thank those persons who have helped to make this effort possible, including Verne Ray, vice president of

TAB Books; my colleagues, past and present, including Professors Del Brinkman, John Bremner, Gary Mason and William Seymour of the William Allen White School of Journalism, University of Kansas; and James E. Roper, Washington, D.C., who helped me to realize, those many years ago, the challenge and satisfaction of writing good news copy.

David Dary

Contents

Foreword

Some of the first conversations I had with David Dary, when I joined the faculty of the William Allen White School of Journalism in 1970, dealt with the relative merits of broadcast news and print news. Dave had worked in broadcasting, both at the local and network levels, and my professional work was on newspapers, including **The Emporia Gazette**.

During those first months, Dave and I disagreed good naturedly as friends and colleagues. We followed the traditional arguments of print vs broadcasting. Then, we began to discover that we really did not have as much to disagree about as we might have thought. We began to agree with each other about the need for good reporting and good writing and we tended to forget about the differences between broadcasting and print. Although we probably never will completely agree on who can do what best in news reporting, we certainly do agree on the basics of good journalism.

Dave decided to do more than just talk about the need for good reporting and writing by print men and broadcasters. He decided to write a book on reporting which would put emphasis on the similarities between broadcasting and reporting rather than on their differences. This book is the result of that effort. I think Dave has done a fine job of incorporating the thinking of textbook writers, broadcast journalists and print journalists in this book. It should be of termendous value to the beginning journalist, especially if he has not decided whether he wants a career in broadcasting or print journalism. It can also be of great help to the professional who is interested in good reporting and writing first and in what medium he works for second.

Dave has succeeded here with a book that few have attempted to write—a reporting manual for all journalists. He has blended the ideas of the present and the result is a very practical approach to the art of reporting and writing news.

I feel good that perhaps a part of the reason this book was written is the result of those discussions and arguments which Dave and I have had over the past two years. I wish I had written it first. But, Dave has done it and done it well. I hope you find it helpful, both as a guidebook for reporting and as a bridge between print and broadcast journalism.

Del Brinkman

Associate Professor
William Allen White School
        of Journalism
University of Kansas
Lawrence, Kansas

Chapter 1

The News Media

A people without reliable news is, sooner or later, a people without the basis of freedom.

Harold J. Laski

It is not known just when the first news story was communicated. It may have been one caveman telling another of an attack by a dinosaur. It is known that about 454 B.C., Julius Caesar, Roman consul, ordered daily written reports of the activities of the Roman senate. These news reports, called **Acta Diurna**, were posted for Roman citizens to read. However, such reports were few in number. Each was hand written. Printing had not yet been discovered.

THE DEVELOPMENT OF PRINTING

Long ago some human being inked the surface of a raised design and pressed it against another surface, discovering printing. However, history does not record exactly when that happened or who did it. It is known that wood-block printing was developed in China some time before 770 A.D. when the Chinese carved words and pictures on wood blocks by hand.

About 1040 A.D., Pi Sheng, a Chinese printer, made movable type out of clay. He used a separate piece of type for each letter that he printed. But movable type did not become popular in China because the language had several thousand separate characters. Too many pieces of type were required. The Chinese found it easier and less expensive to print from carved wood blocks.

THE FIRST NEWSPAPERS

With the invention of printing came the newspaper and the first major medium of mass communication. What may have been the world's first paper was **Tsing Pao**, a court journal published in Peking, China. Its exact starting date is unknown, but it began about 500 A.D. and continued until 1935. Carved blocks were used to produce the first copies.

Two centuries later, in 700 A.D., the **Ching Pao**, a silk newspaper, appeared. Not quite three centuries later the **Peking Gazette** was born. It also was a court paper. First published in 1350, it is the first printed daily paper of which there is any record.

Newspapers in Europe

Before printing developed in Europe in the 15th century, minstrels composed songs about current happenings and traveled the countryside carrying the news. In many cities and towns the news was carried from house to house by town criers. But these methods of "telling the news" gradually faded after Johann Gutenberg introduced movable type in Europe about 1440. Gutenberg combined movable type with two other developments—the printing press (probably adapted from a wine or cheese press), and ink. These developments lead to the establishment of single-page newspapers.

The first such paper was printed at Nuremburg, Germany, in 1454. Similar news sheets (they were called **conrantos**), containing foreign news exclusively, also appeared in Belgium and England, but they were slow to arrive in England.

Although William Caxton had set up the first printing press in England in 1476, the Crown, from the beginning, carefully regulated printing. And it was in Holland, rather than in England, that the first news sheets printed in English appeared. The first such news sheet was published in December 1620. It contained an account of the battle of Weissenberg, the beginning of the Thirty Years' War.

The First English Newspapers

Historians consider **The Weekly Newes** to have been the first bonafide English newspaper. It was published in London in 1622. The first daily newspaper printed in English was **The**

Daily Courant, published at London in 1702. Its start marked the beginning of newspaper journalism as we know it today.

Before **The Daily Courant** began publication, newspapers printed almost anything, including rumors. However, **The Daily Courant** soon established a different policy after Samuel Buckley took over its operation from Elizabeth Mallet, the paper's founder. She established the paper, but it lasted only a few days under her direction. When Buckley took charge, he insisted that it contain factual news, not just rumors and opinion. Buckley published the newspaper six days a week, sold advertising and became very successful.

The First American Newspaper

The birthplace of journalism in America was Boston, where Benjamin Harris published **Publick Occurrences Both Forreign and Domestick** in 1960. It was the first newspaper in America, but it did not last. The paper was suppressed by the colonial governor, because Harris was unpopular with the authorities and because he had no license to publish. (See Fig. 1-1.)

In colonial times, between 1686 and 1730, each colonial governor had the right to regulate the press. A license was required to publish a newspaper. It was not until 1704, 14 years after Harris' paper failed, that a newspaper was licensed in America. The paper was the **Boston News-Letter** established by John Campbell, a Scotsman and postmaster of Boston, who started the venture by copying news items from English papers. Campbell sent these items in the form of a newsletter to all of the governors of the New England colonies. The News-Letter became so popular that Campbell decided to publish it weekly in printed form and circulate it to the public.

The **Boston News-Letter** was a single sheet of paper printed on both sides. It contained foreign news almost exclusively as did most other early newspapers in Europe and America. Local events appeared only in the form of advertisements. (See Fig. 1-2.)

In an effort to solicit advertising, Campbell wrote in the first issue of his News-Letter:

This News-Letter is to be continued Weekly; and all Persons who have any Houses, Lands, Tenements, Farms, Ships, Vessels, Goods, Wares, or Merchandizes, Ec. to be Sold, or Lett; or Servants

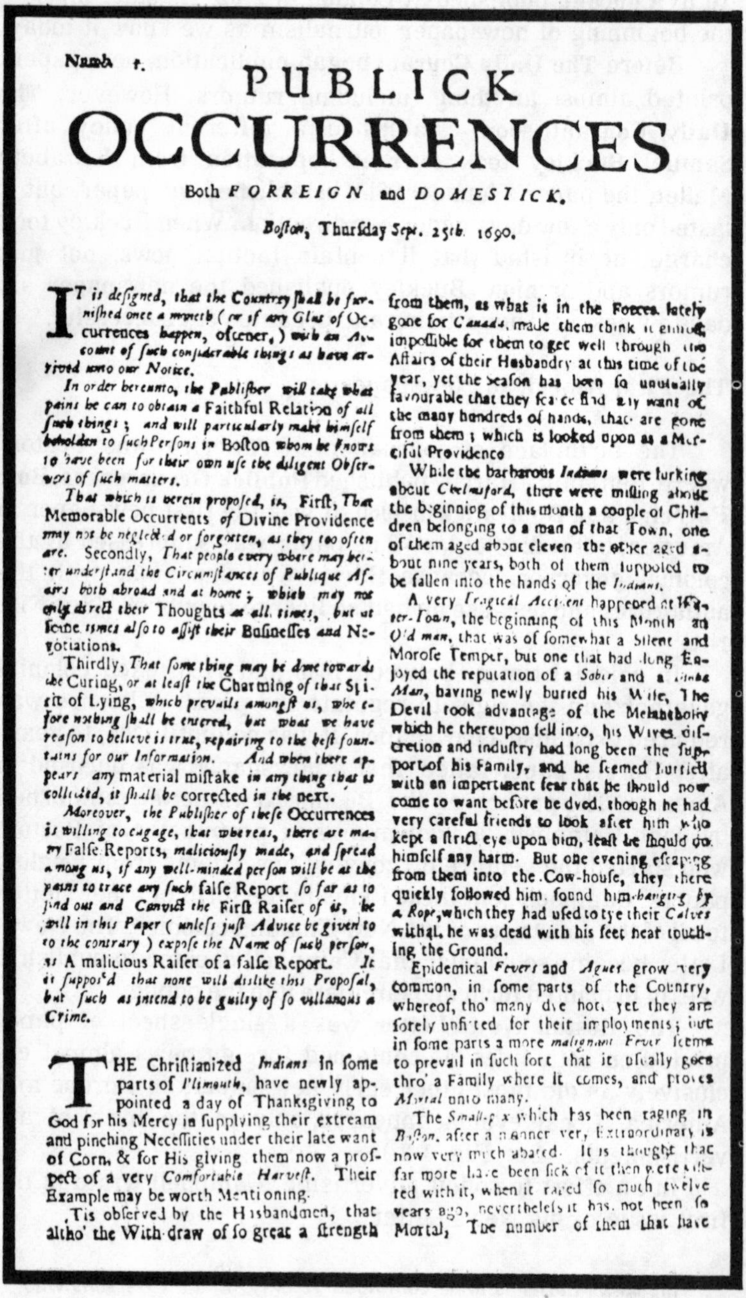

PUBLICK
OCCURRENCES

Both *FORREIGN* and *DOMESTICK.*

Boston, Thursday *Sept.* 25th. 1690.

IT is designed, that the *Country shall be furnished once a moneth* (or if any Glut of Occurrences happen, oftener,) *with an Account of such considerable things as have arrived unto our Notice.*

In order hereunto, the Publisher will take what pains he can to obtain a Faithful Relation of all such things; and will particularly make himself beholden to such Persons in Boston whom he knows to have been for their own use the diligent Observers of such matters.

That which is herein proposed, is, First, *That Memorable Occurrents of Divine Providence may not be neglected or forgotten, as they too often are.* Secondly, *That people every where may better understand the Circumstances of Publique Affairs both abroad and at home; which may not only direct their Thoughts at all times, but at some times also to assist their Businesses and Negotiations.*

Thirdly, *That some thing may be done towards the Curing, or at least the Charming of that Spirit of Lying, which prevails amongst us, wherefore nothing shall be entered, but what we have reason to believe is true, repairing to the best fountains for our Information. And when there appears any material mistake in any thing that is collected, it shall be corrected in the next.*

Moreover, the Publisher of these Occurrences is willing to engage, that whereas, there are many False Reports, maliciously made, and spread among us, if any well-minded person will be at the pains to trace any such false Report so far as to find out and Convict the First Raiser of it, he will in this Paper (unless just Advice be given to to the contrary) expose the Name of such person, as A malicious Raiser of a false Report. It is supposed that none will dislike this Proposal, but such as intend to be guilty of so villanous a Crime.

THE Christianized *Indians* in some parts of *Plimouth,* have newly appointed a day of Thanksgiving to God for his Mercy in supplying their extream and pinching Necessities under their late want of Corn, & for His giving them now a prospect of a very *Comfortable Harvest.* Their Example may be worth Mentioning.

'Tis observed by the Husbandmen, that altho' the With-draw of so great a strength from them, as what is in the Forces lately gone for *Canada,* made them think it almost impossible for them to get well through the Affairs of their Husbandry at this time of the year, yet the season has been so unusually favourable that they scarce find any want of the many hundreds of hands, that are gone from them; which is looked upon as a Merciful Providence.

While the barbarous *Indians* were lurking about *Chelmsford,* there were missing about the beginning of this month a couple of Children belonging to a man of that Town, one of them aged about eleven the other aged about nine years, both of them supposed to be fallen into the hands of the *Indians.*

A very *Tragical Accident* happened at *Water-Town,* the beginning of this Month an *Old man,* that was of somewhat a Silent and Morose Temper, but one that had long Enjoyed the reputation of a *Sober* and a *pious Man,* having newly buried his Wife, The Devil took advantage of the Melancholly which he thereupon fell into, his Wives discretion and industry had long been the support of his Family, and he seemed hurried with an impertinent fear that he should now come to want before he dyed, though he had very careful friends to look after him who kept a strict eye upon him, least he should do himself any harm. But one evening escaping from them into the Cow-house, they there quickly followed him, found him hanging by a Rope, which they had too tye their Calves withal, he was dead with his feet near touching the Ground.

Epidemical *Fevers* and *Agues* grow very common, in some parts of the Country, whereof, tho' many die not, yet they are sorely unfitted for their imployments; but in some parts a more *malignant Fever* seems to prevail in such sort that it usually goes thro' a Family where it comes, and proves *Mortal* unto many.

The *Small-pox* which has been raging in *Boston,* after a manner very *Extraordinary* is now very much abated. It is thought that far more have been sick of it then were visited with it, when it raged so much twelve years ago, nevertheless it has not been so *Mortal,* The number of them that have

Fig. 1-1. The first colonial newspaper in America, **Publick Occurrences**, was published in 1690. It was banned after one issue.

Runaway; or Goods Stoll or Lost, may have the same Inserted at a Reasonable Rate; from Twelve Pence to Five Shillings, and not to exceed.

The next newspaper to appear in America was **The Boston-Gazette**, first published in 1719. Two years later James Franklin, the older brother of Benjamin Franklin, established the **New England Courant**. James Franklin's paper was the first in America to criticize authorities. Franklin soon was sent to jail where he served one month. However, the paper continued publication and lasted until 1726 when Franklin moved away. It was at the **New England Courant** where Benjamin Franklin learned the printing trade.

REPORTING LOCAL NEWS

Until the **American Weekly Mercury** was founded at Philadelphia in 1719 (it was the third newspaper published in the colonies), American newspapers contained no local news other than that appearing as paid advertising. There was little need to report local happenings, since communities were small and everyone knew what was going on. But under the leadership of Andrew Bradford, the **American Weekly Mercury** emphasized local news in Philadelphia, then a city of several thousand persons.

During the 18th century most American newspapers followed what some historians call the "history-concept" of news. Deaths of important persons, wars, large storms, celebrations and the movements of the colonial governors were the types of stories covered by the majority of America's newspapers. But John Peter Zenger and his **New York Weekly Journal** went further.

John Peter Zenger

John Peter Zenger established **The New York Weekly Journal** in 1733 to aid the popular party that was struggling with the tyrannical colonial governors. Zenger editorially opposed British authority. In so doing, he established newspapers as an important factor in influencing public opinion on the important social, economic and political questions of the day.

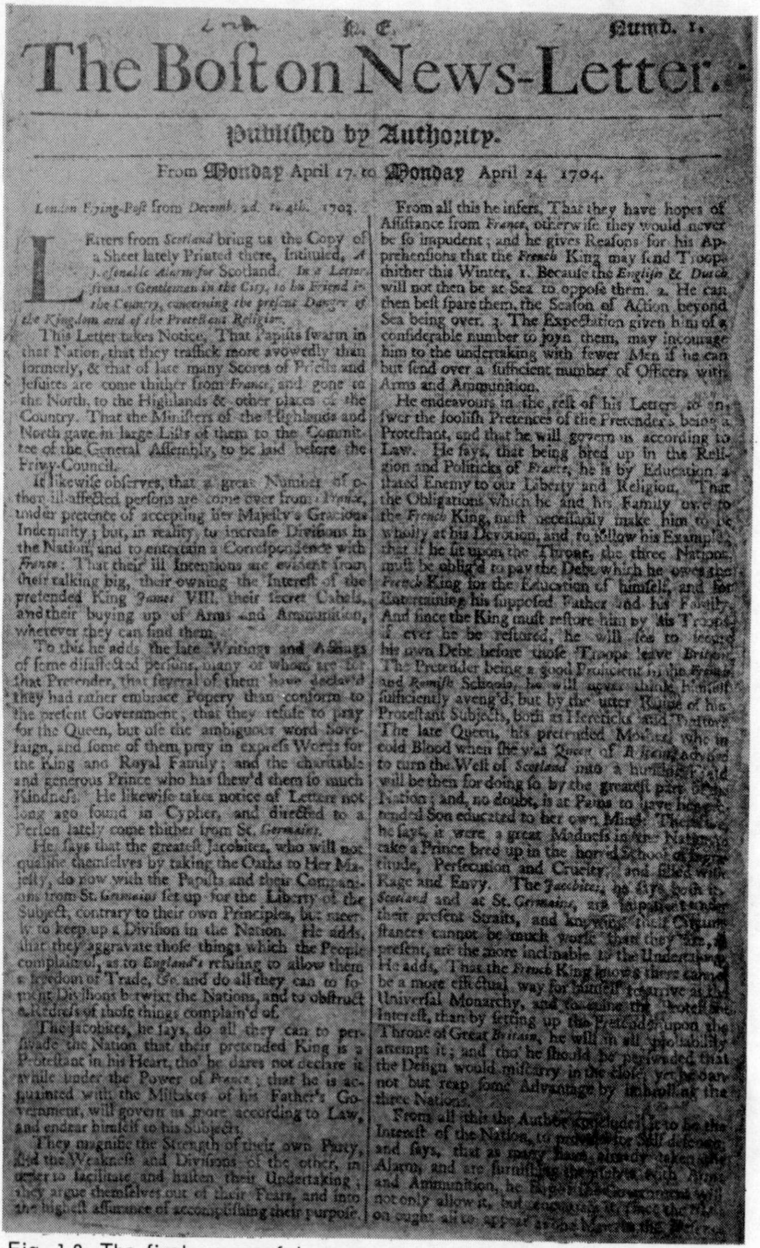

Fig. 1-2. The first successful newspaper in America, John Campbell's **Boston News-Letter,** established in 1704. This photograph shows the front page of issue number one. Notice the phrase "Published by Authority" on the masthead. In the early 18th century newspapers were required to have a license to publish.

But Zenger's criticism of the colonial governor led to his arrest in November 1734 on charges of seditious libel. In the trial that followed, Zenger was successfully defended by Andrew Hamilton, a Philadelphia lawyer, in what is today considered the first great legal test of press freedom. The case involved the right of the press to criticize the government. The jury's verdict of not guilty established a precedent that influenced later court decisions and legislation.

NINETEENTH CENTURY AMERICAN NEWSPAPERS

By the early 19th century (1814), the steam engine had been adapted to the printing press and printing was speeded up. Other improvements in printing enabled the growing number of newspapers in the east to increase their circulation and, in turn, disseminate news to more people. More and more Americans turned to newspapers for news which by then included local, national and foreign developments.

Advent of Telegraphy

From the beginning, newspapers relied on personal communication for news. Information was passed along by word of mouth or by written communication. This changed in 1844.

On May 25, 1844, Samuel F. B. Morse sent a message in code from the old Supreme Court Chamber in Washington, D.C. In Baltimore, Morse's assistant decoded the sounds. The message: "What hath God wrought?" Later that day Morse sent the first telegraphic message to be published in a newspaper, the **Baltimore Patriot**. The message told of a vote in the House of Representatives on the Oregon question. Morse's telegraph was a success.

The invention of the telegraph by Morse brought about a whole new system of communication. Newspapers were quick to make use of the telegraph. It stimulated the growth of newspapers in the smaller cities and towns westward to Missouri. By the late 1850s, the telegraph was used by most daily newspapers.

MODERN NEWSPAPERS ESTABLISHED

Between 1833 and 1900, the forerunners of the modern American newspapers were established. The first such paper was the **New York Sun**, a daily, started in 1833 by Benjamin Henry Day. He inaugurated street sales and sold the paper for one penny.

Until the **New York Sun** began, nearly all American newspapers were sold by subscription. Day revolutionized newspaper publishing and, to some extent, news reporting. Day placed much emphasis on human-interest news. His paper was so successful that many imitations were established.

James Gordon Bennett set up the **Morning Herald** in 1835 in New York City and produced a paper that was lively, saucy and spicy. Bennett was one of the first editors to exploit criminal trials and scandals. His paper also was a leader in the development of illustrations and headlines. Bennett forgot an earlier urge to use his newspaper for political influence. Instead, he helped to develop the idea of objective and unbiased news reporting, plus a more lively style of news writing.

Dissatisfaction with the **Herald** by conservative and respectable elements in New York City led Horace Greeley to establish the **New York Tribune** in 1841. Greeley followed a policy of giving readers a newspaper "not merely for a morning glance, but for an evening fireside hour if they can command the time."

Believing it was an editor's duty to take a position on important matters, Greeley sought to improve society through his editorials, proclaiming his convictions of truth without regard to the consequences. Greeley was the first editor to show clearly that it was possible to maintain a thoroughly successful newspaper without depending upon scandal to secure and hold a large circulation.

What many historians consider the beginning of truly impersonal news reporting came with the founding of the **New York Times** in 1851 by Henry J. Raymond. His paper provided news that was not sensational. Although Raymond was a politician, he never used his newspaper to promote personal aspirations.

NEWSPAPERS IN THE WEST

The 1850s and '60s saw the spread of journalism through much of the western frontier. Newspapers appeared in

Nebraska, the Dakotas, Montana, Wyoming, Colorado and Kansas. (See Fig. 1-3.)

The Kansas-Nebraska Act of 1854 brought journalism to "bleeding Kansas." Newspapers appeared as towns were being built. No newspaper remained neutral on the question of slavery. Editors either opposed or favored slavery. Many newspaper plants were burned by opposing forces during the years just prior to the Civil War.

NINETEENTH CENTURY EDITORS

Kansas produced many outstanding newspapermen including William Allen White, editor of the **Emporia Gazette**. One of White's best known editorials was published on August 20, 1896, entitled: "What's the Matter with Kansas?" It was an angry blast at the Populists, the whiners, do-nothings and the pitiable candidates proposed to represent the State of Kansas. White's editorial was echoed throughout the nation and became a Republican war-cry, not because of what it said about Kansas, but because of its basic philosophies.

Another well known editor was Charles A. Dana, who became editor of the **New York Sun** in 1868. Dana was responsible, in part, for an improved news writing style. He encouraged original, clever and concise writing with emphasis on clarity and condensation. His efforts helped to develop an American style of journalistic writing which was much lighter than the heavier news style used in England. Dana placed emphasis upon the importance of human-interest stories as well as informational news.

One newspaperman who contributed much to the development of western journalism was William Rockhill Nelson (Fig. 1-4), who established the **Kansas City Star** in 1880. Nelson felt it was the reporter's responsibility to write truthfully and entertainingly and also to investigate matters of public concern. Nelson demonstrated that a newspaper could help to make a better community. Nelson did not believe in sensationalism. The newspaper he established nearly 100 years ago continues today as the **Kansas City Star** and **Times**.

There were other prominent newspapermen during the late 19th and early 20th century, including Joseph Pulitzer, who purchased the **New York World** in 1883 and injected the element of crusading into both the newspaper's news and

Fig. 1-3. Journalism on the western frontier was no "bed of roses." This building housed the Kingman, Kansas, **Mercury** in 1880. (Courtesy Kansas State Historical Society.)

Fig. 1-4. William Rockhill Nelson, founder of **The Kansas City Star**. Unlike other great figures of journalism before him, Nelson was not a writer. He believed that the reporter was the heart of the newspaper. He sought the best news editors and editorial writers. Nelson died in 1915. (Courtesy The Kansas City Star.)

editorials; William Randolph Hearst, whose newspapers have been unequaled in their sensationalism in both content and makeup; the Scripps brothers (George H., and James E.), and a cousin, John Scripps Sweeney, whose middle western newspapers included the **Cleveland Press, St. Louis Chronicle, Cincinnati Post** and the **Kentucky Post**; and Adolph S. Ochs, who became publisher of the **New York Times** in 1896. Ochs revived the then declining newspaper. And it was Ochs who adopted the slogan "All the News That's Fit to Print" for the **New York Times**.

Between 1880 and 1900, the number of daily newspapers in the United States increased from 850 to 1,967. By 1910 the number of dailies had increased to 2,200, and in that year there were 11,802 weekly newspapers.

Between 1910 and through 1914, the number of newspapers in the country, and their combined circulation, reached an all-time high. There was no question that the newspaper had become the prime mass medium for communicating news.

THE NEWS MAGAZINE

A new means of communicating news developed in the early 1920s—the news magazine. Although magazines had been around for years, most had been concerned with providing entertainment and opinion. When **Time** magazine was established in 1923 by two young men in their 20s—Henry R. Luce and Briton Hadden—the weekly news magazine was born. In announcing their new magazine, Luce and Hadden noted:

"Although daily journalism has been more highly developed in the United States than in any other country in the world, although foreigners marvel at the excellence of our periodicals, **World's Work, Century, Literary Digest, Outlook,** and the rest, people in America are, for the most part, poorly informed. This is not the fault of the daily newspapers; they print all the news. It is not the fault of the weekly "reviews"; they adequately develop and comment on the news. To say with the facile cynic that it is the fault of the people themselves is to beg the question. People are uninformed because no publication has adapted itself to the time which busy men are able to spend on simply keeping informed."

For its readers, **Time** organized and departmentalized the news. The magazine's slogan became, "Time is written as if by one man for one man." By 1929, **Time** had a circulation of 200,000.

In the years that followed, other successful magazines were established, including **Newsweek,** founded in 1933; **U. S. News & World Report,** part of which was established in 1929; and **Business Week,** started in 1929.

THE DEVELOPMENT OF RADIO BROADCASTING

The development of radio broadcasting was the natural continuation of technology following the invention of the telegraph and telephone. Much of the credit for radio, or "wireless," as it was first called, goes to Guglielmo Marconi, an Italian, who conceived the idea of wireless telegraphy. He first transmitted Morse code on his own, sending and receiving equipment from his father's garden in Italy. In 1896, he moved to England, took out a patent for his invention and formed a radio company.

By 1899, Marconi was sending messages across the English Channel. Two years later he successfully sent signals from England to Newfoundland. By 1902, trans-Atlantic messages were exchanged, using the Morse code. Marconi opened regular telegraph service between Europe and America in 1910, followed two years later by the first trans-Pacific telegraph service between San Francisco and Hawaii.

Transmitting the Human Voice

The inventions of two men were responsible for the development of voice communication by radio. In 1904, John Ambrose Fleming, an English electrical engineer, invented the 2-element vacuum tube that could detect radio signals. About two years later, Lee De Forest, an American, produced the 3-element electron tube which made sound transmission possible.

With the aid of these milestone developments, radio voice communication was born. Within a few years, hundreds of home-built radio transmitters were in operation across the United States. Nearly all were experimental stations, with the exception of a few used for communication by shipping companies and the military.

Fig. 1-5. Paul W. White, CBS Radio's first news director (center), speaks into a microphone during a CBS election news broadcast in 1944. The man to White's right is Robert Trout. The other persons are not identified. (Courtesy CBS.)

First Radio Broadcasting Station

Until the late 1950s, most historians credited either WWJ, Detroit, Michigan, or KDKA, Pittsburgh, Pennsylvania, with having been the first radio station to transmit regular programs in 1920. In the late '50s, however, evidence was uncovered to show that, in fact, the first radio broadcast station went on the air with regular programs in 1909 at San Jose, California. The station was built and operated by Dr. Charles David Herrold, principal of the Herrold College of Engineering and Wireless. It was located in the Garden Bank Building at San Jose.

Thinking that radio might be used to reach large audiences, Dr. Herrold distributed crystal sets in his neighborhood. He then broadcast news and music to his neighbors. His news programs were crude by today's standards, but his concept of radio broadcasting has changed little in more than half a century. What originally was Herrold's station is today KCBS, the 50,000-watt key CBS station in San Francisco.

RADIO NEWS

As radio broadcasting grew during the early 1920s, many stations broadcast news programs. But most such programs were aired by newspapermen who broadcast newspaper stories. Radio stations could not afford to gather their own news, nor would the press associations, controlled by the newspapers, sell news to radio.

After the radio networks were formed in the late 1920s, radio became prosperous. By the early '30s, network radio could afford to buy press association news, but the Associated Press, United Press and the International News Service would not sell to radio.

In 1933, CBS decided to gather its own news. A former United Press editor, Paul W. White (Fig. 1-5), was hired to head the Columbia News Service. For several months the service was successful, but many newspaper publishers objected to the competition. Early in 1934, the Columbia News Service stopped gathering domestic news.

Radio news did not mature until World War II. By then the three major press associations were selling news to radio, and radio reporters also were gathering news at home and over-

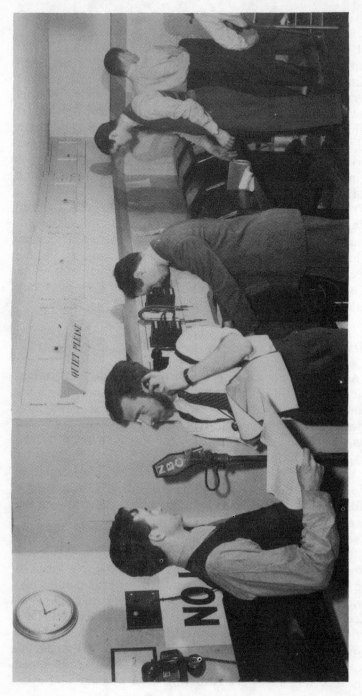

Fig. 1-6. NBC's Robert St. John stands to the right of the NBC News microphone ready to broadcast a war bulletin during the early '40s. The scene is the old NBC News wireroom in New York City. (Courtesy NBC.)

seas (Fig. 1-6). Before the war ended, there was increased harmony between newspapers and the radio industry.

TELEVISION NEWS

Although NBC inaugurated America's first regular television service in 1939, it was not until after World War II that television became an important medium for news. NBC began the first regular weeknight television news program in 1948. It was called the "Camel News Caravan" and the anchorman was John Cameron Swayze (Fig. 1-7). CBS followed suit and a few months later entered the TV network news competition with a nightly news program called "Television News with Douglas Edwards."

Television grew at a rapid rate during the late '40s and early '50s, but television news moved slowly. The medium had adapted many radio programs to television, but having a well known radio newsman sit before a mike reading the news was dull television. It was distracting. It was radio with a picture. Television news needed visual news material.

Although the television networks and individual stations experimented with theatrical newsreel film during the late '40s and early '50s, it was not until 1953 that a significant improvement in television news visuals occurred. In that year CBS established its own film gathering service called CBS Newsfilm—news on film. CBS could control the filming of their own news stories. NBC soon established their own news filming service.

By the late 1950s and early '60s, the television networks and many individual stations were expanding their news gathering, reporting and on-air programming of news. Names like Walter Cronkite, Chet Huntley, David Brinkley and others became household words. (See Fig. 1-8.)

In 1965, Elmo Roper and Associates released a survey covering the period 1959 through 1964. It was called **The Public's View of Television and Other Media**. The survey showed that the public was getting most of its news from television.

THE NEWS MEDIA TODAY

Advancements in communication have eliminated the delay that once existed between the time an event occurred

Fig. 1-7. John Cameron Swayze, anchorman of NBC's "Camel News Caravan," network television's first regular weeknight TV news program. Swayze ended each evening's news program with, "That's the story, folks. Glad we could get together." (Courtesy NBC.)

Fig. 1-8. Getting the "who, what, when, where and why" of the story is ABC News correspondent Marlene Sanders on assignment in South Vietnam. (Courtesy ABC.)

and when it was reported. Electronic journalism today produces what might be described as instant news or news as it happens, with the print media following close with detailed reports.

Today, Americans are exposed to more news than ever before. Yet, since 1969, when Vice President Spiro Agnew attacked what he called "the tiny fraternity of privileged men," the news media has been exposed to more criticism than perhaps at any time during the last century. Each one of the news media does have its shortcomings. It is not perfect. But an imperfect product is better than none at all. As Thomas Jefferson wrote in 1786, "Our liberty depends on the freedom of the press, and that cannot be limited without being lost."

SUGGESTED READINGS

The reader with more than a passing interest in journalism history will find additional material in the following books:

Michael J. Arlen, **Living-Room War.** New York: Viking Press, 1969.

David Dary, **Radio News Handbook.** Blue Ridge Summit, Pa.: TAB Books, 1970.

David Dary, **Television News Handbook,** Blue Ridge Summit, Pa.: TAB Books, 1971.

Edwin Emery, **The Press and America.** Englewood Cliffs, N.J.: Prentice-Hall, 1962.

Robert F. Karolevitz, **Newspapering in the Old West.** Seattle: Superior, 1965.

Alexander Kendrick, **Prime Time: The Life of Edward R. Murrow.** Boston: Little-Brown, 1969.

Carl E. Lindstrom, **The Fading American Newspaper.** New York: Doubleday, 1960.

Frank Luther Mott, **American Journalism.** New York: Macmillan, 1949.

William L. Rivers, Theodore Peterson and Jay W. Jensen, **The Mass Media and Modern Society**. San Francisco: Rinehart Press, 1971.

A. A. Schechter with Edward Anthony, **I Live On Air**. New York: Stokes, 1941.

Irving Settel, **A Pictorial History of Radio**. New York: Citadel, 1960.

Irving Settel and William Laas, **A Pictorial History of Television**. New York: Grosset and Dunlap, 1969.

Paul W. White, **News On The Air**. New York, Harcourt-Brace, 1947.

William A. Wood., **Electronic Journalism**. New York: Columbia University Press, 1967.

Chapter 2

What Is News

When a dog bites a man, that's not news, because it happens so often. But if a man bites a dog, that is news.

John Bogart

The word **news** is rooted in Latin, in the old Germanic **new-yo** and in the Old English word **neowe**, meaning something new. During the 16th century the word **newes** in England took on a more limited meaning. By the early 17th century, it was used in the singular to differentiate between the casual dissemination of information and the deliberate attempt to gather and process the latest information of public importance.

"What's the news?" "What's been happening?" "What event may affect my life or the life of someone I know?" "What's the weather going to be today?" "Did my favorite football team win?" Today, these and countless other questions are asked daily by millions of Americans.

Few persons are in the position to learn for themselves everything they would like to know. They simply do not have the time nor the resources to search out all of the information they desire. Therefore, most persons must turn to the news media and the profession that exists to answer these questions—journalism.

JOURNALISM AND NEWS

Journalism means many things to many people. Charles Chapin of the old New York **World** described journalism as the worship of "that inky-nosed, nine-eyed, clay-footed god called news." Matthew Arnold called journalism "literature in a hurry," while Stanley Walker, the late city editor of the **New York Herald-Tribune**, said journalism is composed of "women, wampum, and wrongdoing." And there are many other colorful definitions of journalism. In its own way each is correct, but for our purposes journalism will be considered as the collecting, writing, editing, and dissemination of news.

Historically, journalism has involved the reporting of news, but it also has been involved in the interpretation of news and the dissemination of opinion based on the news. At times journalism may entertain, but its prime function is to provide the raw material on which readers, listeners, and viewers can form their opinions.

In the United States, journalism is independent. It must be, in a democracy, if it is to seek out truth above all things, and present the truth with fairness, without error, bias, and prejudice. Journalism is the only private business enterprise protected by the Constitution; thus, it is more responsible to the public than most other businesses.

NEWS DEFINED

Every dictionary and nearly all journalism textbooks contain definitions of the word **news**. Most are accurate, but few are alike because the word "news" means many things to many people.

News is a constantly changing property, a highly perishable commodity. A story that is described as news at one hour may not be news two hours later. The value of a news story changes with time. One definition of news that relates to both print and broadcast is:

> News is any reliable and unbiased report of an event containing timely or hitherto unknown information that affects the lives, welfare, future, or interest of the readers, listeners, or viewers receiving the report.

In this definition the word **report** is used in a very broad sense and includes written, oral, and visual material, including motion picture film (newsfilm). This definition makes it clear that news is the account of an event, not the event itself.

THE NATURE OF NEWS

A man picks up the morning newspaper and scans the headlines. Suddenly a headline catches his attention. He reads the story with interest.

Across town a housewife turns on her radio to learn what has happened overnight. As the woman prepares breakfast she pays only passing attention to the news. Then the newsman begins to tell about an overnight fire at a local department store. The woman's attention is suddenly caught. She concentrates on the news story. She is interested.

What causes such **interest** in news? What are the psychological processes that determine a reader's or listener's interest in news? One explanation was given in 1949 by Wilbur Schramm, an authority on communication, writing in **Journalism Quarterly**:

"I think it is self-evident that a person selects news in expectation of a reward. This reward may be either of two kinds. One is related to what Freud calls the Pleasure Principle, the other to what he calls the Reality Principle. For want of better names, we shall call these two classes **immediate reward** and **delayed reward**.

"In general, the kinds of news which may be expected to furnish immediate reward are news of crime and corruption, accidents and disasters, sports and recreation, social events and human interest. Delayed reward may be expected from news of public affairs, economic matters, social problems, science, education, and health.

"News of the first kind pays its rewards at once. A reader can enjoy a vicarious experience without any of the dangers or stresses involved. He can shiver luxuriously at an axe murder, shake his head sympathetically and safely at a tornado, identify himself with the winning team or (herself) with the society lady who wore a well described gown at the reception for Lady Morganbilt, laugh understandingly (and from superior knowledge) at a warm little story of children or dogs.

"News of the second kind, however, pays its rewards later. It sometimes requires the reader to endure unpleasantness or annoyances—as, for example, when he reads of the ominous foreign situation, the mounting national debt, rising taxes, falling market, scarce housing, cancer, epidemics, farm blights. It has a kind of "threat value." It is read so that as the reader selects delayed reward news, he jerks himself into the world of surrounding reality to which he can adapt himself only by hard work. When he selects news of the other kind, he retreats usually from the world of threatening reality toward the dream world."

BACKGROUND NEWS

"Everything changes but change," wrote Israel Zangwill, a British novelist and dramatist. Certainly journalism is no exception. In 1922, Walter Lippman, writing in **Public Opinion**, said that news is "but the report of an aspect that has obtruded itself. The news does not tell you how the seed is germinating in the ground, but it may tell you when the first sprout breaks through the surface."

Before the early 1920s, this was true. Newspapers generally limited their reporting to overt acts. However, reporting gradually changed. Between the 1920s and the '40s, newspapers began to do more than just report overt news. They started reporting facts that indicated when something was going to happen. They began to look below the surface for the hidden news and for background information that would be of interest to their readers. Newspapers began reporting stories about people and events and the changes that were occurring in society.

Radio, in part, was responsible for this change. When radio stations began reporting news, the newspapers found they had competition that could deliver the news faster. The newspaper monopoly in news was challenged. But then some newspaper editors realized that radio could not take the time to report detailed news. The newspapers could. And by the time television arrived in the late 1940s, many newspapers were devoting considerable space to background news.

Today, the practice continues, but broadcast journalists are also reporting more background news through documentary programs and other forms of news broadcasting.

ELEMENTS OF NEWS

The form in which an event is reported is called a **news story**. Every news story contains facts. These facts usually answer such questions as **who, what, when, where, why,** and **how.** But facts alone are not news. It is what the facts mean to those persons receiving them that determines whether an account of an event is news. If a group of facts makes news, one or more of the elements of news must be present. There are five main elements:

(1) **Timeliness:** As a general rule, the fresher the story the better. The public today demands fresh news. Competition within the news media requires that fresh news be delivered. Such news usually deals with current events or is seasonal in nature. Consider the following example which appeared in the **San Francisco Examiner:**

> Seven people, including two children, were routed from a handsome turn-of-the-century frame building in Cow Hollow early this morning by a two-alarm fire that gutted the top floor.
>
> A large crowd was attracted by the blaze, which began about 5:45 a.m. from undetermined causes in the attic of the home of Mr. and Mrs. Michael Hogan at 3028 Laguna St.
>
> The Hogans, with their children, Traven, 4, and Daisy, 3, and three adult guests left the burning building without injury, but fireman Jerry Overstreet, 35, of the rescue squad was treated at Central Emergency Hospital for cuts and burns on his hands.
>
> Assistant Chief Joseph Schneider estimated damage at $12,000.

This story occurred the same day the story was published. The event was news, in part, because it was fresh. But the story contains other elements of news.

(2) **Proximity:** Usually, if readers or listeners are geographically close to a story, there is more interest. The fire story, published by the **San Francisco Examiner,** is a case in point. Many readers in the San Francisco area probably were interested in the story because it occurred in their area. The same story, however, would have been of little interest in Atlanta, Georgia, or elsewhere outside the San Francisco area. It is only natural that people are interested in what goes on in their own communities.

(3) **Prominence:** Events involving prominent persons, places, and things may be news. If your neighbor gets into a fight with another neighbor and the police are called, the story may make the local newspaper or be broadcast by the local radio station. But unless one of the neighbors involved is prominent, there will be little interest in the story outside of your neighborhood. But let a prominent person get into a fight and the event is big news. An example is the following story carried by the Associated Press on its national newspaper and broadcast wires datelined Portland, Oregon:

> Raquel Welch suffered a cut lip and swollen face when she and another actress "got carried away" while filming a fight, according to a spokesman for Metro-Goldwyn-Mayer.

He named the other actress involved in the incident as Helena Kallianiotes.

"What happened? She got slugged," the spokesman explained.

Miss Welch plays a roller derby star in an MGM production titled "Kansas City Bomber."

When she would be able to resume work was not immediately known.

(4) **Affect:** If an account of an event affects the lives, welfare or future of the persons receiving the report, it is news, even if the story occurred thousands of miles distant. Consider the following Associated Press story concerning President Nixon's 1972 trip to Russia:

MOSCOW (AP) - President Nixon and Communist Party Chief Leonid Brezhnev signed a joint statement of long-range principles today agreeing to avoid military confrontations and envisioning eventual total world disarmament.

For the nearer future, Nixon and the Soviet leader agreed in a companion communique to hold a European security conference—long a goal of the Soviet regime—quite soon.

The conference will aim first at providing for an East-West cutback in military forces in Central Europe, notably those in East and West Germany.

Although this story occurred on the other side of the world, Americans were interested because it appeared to signal the end of the arms race and perhaps the Cold War, and because it also involved the President of the United States.

(5) **Human Interest:** This element probably appears in more news stories than any other. Human beings are interested in what other human beings say and do. Each example thus far presented in this chapter has, to some degree, contained human interest. Now read the following story carried by Reuter, the British news service, and published by **The Christian Science Monitor,** datelined Neath, Wales:

Tim the terrier took a big bite of his master's old hat—and was rescued from a deep mountainside crevice where he had been trapped for four days.

When all attempts to widen the crevice with earth-moving equipment had failed, someone thought of lowering Danny Evans's battered knit cap on a 60-foot rope. Tim took a firm hold and was pulled out, happy and unhurt.

Is the story of a dog being rescued in Wales news in the United States? In this case, the answer is yes. The story had much appeal to readers and listeners. The story's main ingredients are human interest and emotion. And it is the public's reaction to the story that makes this otherwise insignificant story news thousands of miles away.

News often reflects action. Someone does something or something happened. While **what happened** is an important ingredient in any news story, the reaction of the reader or listener to the story must also be considered. Often the **impact** of an otherwise insignificant story will determine whether or not an event is news.

CLASSIFICATION OF NEWS

Nearly all news stories can be placed into one of three broad classifications based on the **time** factor. They are:

(1) **Announcements of scheduled future events:** Trials, elections, legislative hearings, meetings and many other scheduled events fall under this classification. This type of news story tells of an event that has been scheduled but the outcome is unknown. An example of this type of news story appeared in a Kansas daily newspaper, **The Coffeyville Journal:**

> The public hearing to consider proposed modifications in the downtown urban renewal project here is scheduled for 7:30 p.m. today and all interested persons are urged to attend.
>
> The meeting will be conducted in the City Commission room on the second floor of City Hall.
>
> Expected to make presentations and answer any questions are UR Agency Executive Director Lynn Goodell and several members of his staff. Coffeyville City Commissioners are expected to attend.
>
> The proposed changes, which basically would result in a lessening of the number of parking lots and a corresponding increase in the number of commercial redevelopment sites downtown, must be acted upon officially by City Commissioners due to funding deadlines imposed by Federal Housing and Urban Development officials.
>
> The revised plan would require about $1.6 million in additional federal funds, Goodell said, but the overall project change would result in a savings to the City of about $2 million due to the decrease in number of public use sites to be acquired and improved.

(2) **Reports of current events:** This type of news tells of an event that has occurred. An example is the Maryland shooting of Alabama Governor George Wallace. Here are the first three paragraphs of the Wallace story as carried by the **Chicago Tribune:**

(From Tribune Wire Service)

LAUREL, Md., May 15 - An assassin fired at least three shots into Gov. George C. Wallace of Alabama at near point-blank range today, seriously wounding him as he campaigned for the Democratic presidential nomination. Reports from the hospital indicated the possibility of serious spinal damage.

At 5 p.m. Chicago time, two hours after the shooting at a shopping center on the eve of Maryland's primary election, Wallace was being prepared for neurosurgery at Holy Cross Hospital in Silver Spring.

"I would say in medical terms, he is alive," said a hospital spokesman. Wallace's press secretary, Billy Joe Camp, described his condition as "serious but stable."

(3) **Events that are likely to happen:** This type of story reveals something that may happen in the future but is, at present, not scheduled. Stories of this nature usually are the result of digging on the part of the reporter. A good example is the following Associated Press newspaper story carried on June 8, 1972:

New York (AP) - Sen. Edmund Muskie, former front-runner for the Democratic presidential nomination, reportedly is ready to support Sen. George McGovern, who is now in first place.

The New York Times said Muskie intimates were saying the Maine senator was leaning toward an endorsement of McGovern during a speech tomorrow to the National Press Club in Washington. NBC said Muskie's "present plans are to announce his support" of the South Dakotan during the speech.

McGovern flew to Washington yesterday and NBC said he is expected to confer there today with Muskie.

This story, however, did not turn out as expected. The next day the Associated Press carried the following:

Washington (AP) - Sen. Edmund Muskie said today he is not going to hand Sen. George McGovern the Democratic presidential nomination, at least until McGovern makes peace with skeptics in the party.

Conceding that McGovern probably will get the nomination anyway, Muskie said he still was not going to give the endorsement and 166 delegates which might make it certain.

In a National Press Club speech, Muskie rejected arguments that he should swing his support to the South Dakota senator in order to blunt a "stop McGovern" movement and prevent a party split.

"Party unity is not achieved with the magic wand of the kingmaker," Muskie said. "No man can hand George McGovern a united party. And I would do him a grave disservice to pretend that I could do so."

While all of the examples used in this chapter appeared in newspapers, the same news elements and the time classification of stories apply to news by radio and television. News is news, regardless of the medium used to disseminate the information.

EXERCISES

1. Select ten news stories from your local newspaper.

a. Using the definition of news presented in this chapter, determine if the stories qualify as news in your community.

b. Examine each story and determine which of the five elements of news appear in each story.

c. Determine the time classification of each story.

2. Select a local radio or television news program. Listen to the news program and list the news stories broadcast. At the end of each story indicate whether you were interested in the story. If so, list the reasons why.

Chapter 3

Gathering News

What you **see** is news,
What you **know** is background,
What you **feel** is opinion.

Lester Markel

The news reporter's job is not to make news. It is to gather and organize in written form those facts that are newsworthy. The reporter is the middle man in the business of news dissemination. He or she must translate facts into meaningful information.

REPORTER'S QUALIFICATIONS

"What does it take to become a news reporter?" "Should a person go to college and major in journalism?" "Is experience on the job better than a college education?" These questions and many more are asked each year by high school graduates interested in following a career in journalism.

There are no easy answers to these questions. Experienced professionals have different opinions. If a newspaper editor worked his way up the ladder from copy boy to reporter and eventually to editor, he may recommend that route. A broadcast newsman who majored in journalism at college may recommend an education at one of several good journalism schools across the country. The answers usually depend upon the experiences of the professional journalists asked to comment. The person interested in journalism will find better answers by examining the somewhat standard qualifications most professional journalists look for when hiring reporters and news writers:

(1) **Personal traits**: The reporter must be an honest and sincere person. He must be dependable and responsible.

Above all he must be interested in people. The individual who does not enjoy meeting and talking with people will not make a good reporter. Successful journalists are interested in what other people do and say, their successes and failures. The reporter must have a wholesome curiosity about life in general.

(2) **Thinking:** The reporter must be a thinker. He is a translater. His job demands careful thought to interpret the meaning of events. Thinking is the heart of news composition. It also is the basis for sound news judgment. The reporter must sift through facts, determine the news, and then mentally plan how to present the material in a clear, fair, and honest style. His attitude must be that of a person detached from an event. The reporter must be skeptical.

(3) **Writing:** The reporter must be a good writer. Good news writing, as mentioned above, goes hand in hand with thinking. Writing news is not mechanical. Whether the reporter works for a newspaper, radio, or television operation, he must be proficient in the use of language, grammar, and so forth. In the case of the broadcast journalist, he may also be required to broadcast news on radio or television. Every successful reporter is proficient with the typewriter.

(4) **Education:** The reporter must have a broad education. The very nature of news demands that the reporter have perspective and an understanding of the forces that shape our society and the world. A broad college education is desired.

WHERE NEWS COMES FROM

The wholesaler in the process of news dissemination is the **news source**. The dictionary defines a source as one who supplies information. If that information is accurate, current, and has some effect on the lives, welfare, future, or interest of those persons receiving the report, it usually is considered to be news.

The news reporter, regardless of the medium in which he works, must have reliable news sources. The number of such sources and how much information they provide are factors that determine, in part, the quality of news coverage by any newspaper, radio or television, or CATV operation.

LOCAL NEWS SOURCES

The news director of a small Kansas radio station said he had 35,000 news sources in his community. Of course, he was referring to the population of his community. Theoretically, he was correct. Every person in any city or town or in any rural area is a potential news source.

When dealing with any news source the reporter should check and recheck the information he receives. Because news reporters gather much news second hand, every story must be verified before it is printed or broadcast.

To make certain a news story is accurate, the reporter should (1) try to get the other side of any story that is controversial; (2) do not guess or take a chance with facts, or figures or names—check them out; (3) watch improbable statements, those that do not ring true—doublecheck; and (4) never be content with the information provided in a news release or that which you receive from only one source. Check different news sources against each other.

NEWS BEATS

The most common method of gathering local news is the news beat. A news beat is the regular assignment of potential news sources to a specific reporter. The reporter is responsible for all news that originates from those sources.

Face-to-face contact with news sources is usually the most productive way of getting information. It can produce an atmosphere in which a news source is likely to discuss more openly the problems and issues of a story. But the reporter must constantly evaluate and verify what his news sources say to make certain the information is accurate. Through the daily contact with news sources, the reporter may become a personal friend of the person or persons involved. While this is perfectly normal, the reporter must make certain he uses information from such sources that are reliable. In large communities, radio and television stations and newspapers usually have several news beats for their reporters. But in small communities one reporter may be able to handle all potential news sources on one beat. It depends upon the size of the community and whether the reporter is gathering news for print or broadcast. The demands vary greatly as do the deadlines and other factors caused by time and the differences within the media.

News beats usually turn up many routine news stories. They also give the imaginative newsman the opportunity to develop feature stories or to investigate rumors or tips. The casual conversation which the reporter holds with a person on his news beat may lead to news. But the reporter should try to keep the conversation casual. News sources usually talk more freely in such an atmosphere. Few experienced reporters begin each round on their news beats with the question, "What's the news today?" The question immediately puts everyone on guard.

INTERVIEWING

Unlike the casual conversation on a street corner, the interview is designed to obtain specific information. The interview is a scheduled meeting requested by a reporter. There are several guidelines that the reporter must follow to make certain that his interviews produce worthwhile information:

(1) **Background**: Before the interview the reporter should learn as much as he can about the person to be interviewed and the subject to be discussed. This is essential if the reporter is to ask sensible questions and obtain the desired information.

Too often a beginning reporter does not arrange an interview with the person who can provide all of the facts desired because the reporter knows the best source is an important person. The reporter may fear that he will be denied the interview, or, if he is not, he will be brushed off. This is not the approach to take. On the contrary, important people, as a rule, are easy to interview. They expect it. Most are willing to be interviewed, and they are sometimes disappointed if not asked for an interview.

(2) **Prepare questions in advance**: If time permits, the reporter should prepare questions in advance. They should be short and to the point, designed to produce the desired information. Such planning before the interview saves time for both the reporter and the person being interviewed.

(3) **Interviewing**: Interviewing is something of an art. At times it is a contest between the reporter and the person being interviewed, who may not want to discuss a particular matter.

It is the reporter's job to draw out the desired information. The reporter must place himself in the position of his readers or listeners and ask those questions which they would want answered. The reporter must limit his questions to the field of the interviewee's competence. If the reporter has not had the opportunity to background himself before the interview, he should not be afraid to ask basic questions such as "How do you spell your name?" or "What is your title?"

If, during an interview, a news source takes the reporter into his confidence, the reporter must not break that trust. If it is broken, the reporter may not get another story from that source.

Interviews do not always result in big stories nor do they always concern major events. Most interviews are routine. However, they often lead to important stories. Take the example of reporter John Franklin, assigned to interview State Senator Joseph Collins back from the state capital for the weekend.

Franklin thinks it will be a routine interview until, on his way to Collins' office, he learns from a friend that Collins is rumored to be having problems with a local party chairman, Jim Hess. At Collins' office, reporter Franklin asks the senator several questions about his health, how things are going in the state capital and about legislation which the senator has proposed. The senator answers all of the questions and begins to relax. Then reporter Franklin asks, "Have you seen Jim Hess lately?"

Senator: "No, not for several weeks."

Reporter: "Do you plan to?"

Senator: "Well, I don't know. I might see him before I go back to the state capital."

Reporter: "What do you plan to talk about?"

Senator: "Uhh...I...I don't know. What do you mean?"

Reporter: "Well sir, people around town are saying that there's some trouble between you and Hess. Is that true?"

Senator: "Well now I wouldn't call it trouble, just a misunderstanding, I suppose."

Reporter: "Senator, what kind of misunderstanding?"

Senator: "Oh, it's about that new bypass the state wants to put around the town. Hess wants it to go around the south side of town. I don't think it should. Too many people will have to move out."

Reporter: "Where do you think it should go?"

Senator: "If they put it around the north side of town, only a couple of families will be affected, and the cost of the construction would be cheaper, too."

Reporter: "How much would the state save by putting it around the north side?"

Senator: "From what I've heard from the state highway boys, about $100,000. You see, if it's on the north side they wouldn't have to make as many cuts through the hills, the ground is flatter."

Reporter: "Well then, why does Hess want it on the south side?"

Senator: "I'm not really sure. He hasn't told me. But, I'll tell you something, and I don't want you to quote me, but I recall that Hess's wife used to own quite a piece of land on the south edge of town. I don't know if she still does, but if so, I suspect that may be why Hess doesn't like my proposal to put the highway on the north side.

With this information, reporter Franklin felt he had the ingredients for a good story. He thanked Senator Collins and left. At the newsroom Franklin called the state highway department at the state capital. They verified what Senator Collins had said. Then Franklin called Hess who refused to make any comment on the matter. Hess hung up on Franklin.

Reporter Franklin then went to the county courthouse, checked on property ownership on the south side and found that Hess's wife did, in fact, own some 40 acres of land along the southern edge of town. If the highway were built there, land values would probably go up. The result of Franklin's careful questioning of Senator Collins plus the follow-up work, double-checking the facts, gave reporter Franklin a good news story of interest to his community.

USING THE TELEPHONE

The telephone is an important tool for the reporter. It can save time. It has another advantage. When a reporter has a news source on the telephone, he has the full attention of the person on the other end of the line. Quite often a reporter can hold a news source longer on the phone than in person. But unless the reporter is acquainted with the person to whom he is talking, it is better to have face-to-face contact. It is more personal.

In situations where a reporter is responsible for checking many news sources daily, a telephone news beat is sometimes used. After establishing a working relationship in personal visits, the reporter may use the telephone to contact those sources. However, the reporter should try to visit his news sources frequently to maintain personal contact.

Telephone news beats are used more, as a rule, by radio and television news operations than by newspapers. Broadcast news operations usually have fewer reporters than do newspapers. And with more frequent deadlines, the broadcast journalist finds that the telephone saves much time. A typical telephone news beat list for the broadcast newsroom appears in Fig. 3-1.

PRESS-NEWS CONFERENCE

The press or news conference is another means of obtaining information. The press conference was originated early in this century to give newspapermen access to prominent persons who did not have time to meet individually with reporters. Since the 1950s, the term "news conference" has been used more and more to describe such meetings. Broadcast journalists contend that the term "press conference" excludes electronic journalists and implies that only print newsmen are present.

The press-news conference can be requested by a news source or by reporters. If the news source calls the conference, he may want to release information. If reporters ask for a conference with a news source, it is because they want to ask questions of the source.

Although the press-news conference format is used extensively by the President, governors and other high-level officials, it has become commonplace in many cities and towns where anyone from a visiting Hollywood celebrity to a sports official or star athlete or any public figure may call a news or press conference.

Some reporters frown upon this format as a means of getting news. Some contend that very little real news ever comes out of such conferences. They say that a reporter is not

```
                     Telephone Check List


Police Radio Dispatcher.......................................863-2288
    (Check 20 minutes prior to each major news program.)

Fire Department Radio Dispatcher............................863-4422
    (Check in early morning, before noon news program and
      before late evening news program.)

Highway Patrol........................................(999)-857-2435
    (Check in early morning .)

County Police Radio Dispatcher..............................863-9483
    (Check in early morning for overnight activity and
      prior to each major news program.)

Hospitals.....(ask for emergency room).......................863-9487
    (Check in early morning for overnight activity)    ....863-3495

City Manager's Office..................(call at 10 a.m.).......863-2158

County Manager's Office...............(call at 10:15 a.m.)....863-9480

Fire Chief's Office...................(call at 9:30 a.m.).....863-4425

National Weather Service................................(999)-957-5388

Supt. of Schools......................(call at 10:30 a.m.)....863-7364

Zoo Director.................................................863-7480

County Medical Examiner......................................863-8242

County Courthouse.......................(switchboard).......863-9477

City Offices...........................(switchboard).......863-2150
```

Fig. 3-1. An example of a broadcast newsroom telephone news beat. Many radio and television news operations use the telephone to save time.

going to ask questions about a potentially good story in front of his competitors. Others believe that too many public figures schedule news conferences only to obtain public exposure. Still other reporters feel that real news can come from a news conference. They point out that the news source is under more pressure to give straight answers to questions in the presence of several reporters.

Reporters covering news conferences should follow the same rules of the news interview. However, they should be prepared to follow up on questions asked by other reporters. In situations where reporters are given news releases before the conference, the reporters should carefully digest the information and ask questions not answered in the release.

USING TWO-WAY RADIO COMMUNICATION

Since the late 1950s, more and more radio and television newsrooms have installed two-way radio systems to provide instant communication between reporters and cameramen in the field and personnel in the newsroom. Many newspapers have begun using two-way radios for the same purpose.

Two-way radio communication is particularly valuable in radio news operations. Radio communication not only enables field reporters to talk to the newsroom and for the newsroom to dispatch reporters to news events, but reporters on the scene can broadcast live reports of events. Two-way radio communication enables broadcast stations to make full use of their immediacy capability in news reporting.

USING PUBLIC SERVICE MONITORS

Monitoring local police and fire radio calls is another means of obtaining tips on news stories. It has become common practice for newspapers and radio and television stations to monitor all such radio calls in their community.

Although most such radio traffic deals with routine events, the first word of disasters, major crimes, and serious fires and accidents originates with law enforcement and other public safety agencies that use two-way radio communication. With special receivers, newsrooms can keep abreast of such activity and quickly assign reporters and cameramen to cover the important stories.

STRINGERS

The news stringer, sometimes called correspondent, is a part-time newsman. The stringer lives in the area surrounding the community in which the newspaper or radio or television station is located. The stringer provides news from the area in which he or she lives. A stringer may be a school teacher, auto mechanic, insurance salesman, or farmer.

Many newsrooms provide their stringers with a list of the kinds of stories they **do not** want. Here is an example of a DO NOT COVER list:

1. Ordinary births, deaths, and sickness.

2. Verdicts of average lawsuits unless there is an unusual angle.

3. Minor accidents and fires.

4. Business deals, unless they are of prime importance to your community and surrounding area.

5. School and club notes unless you feel the folks 30 miles away will be interested.

Instead of providing stringers with a list of stories not wanted, some newspapers and radio and television stations provide lists detailing the type of stories to cover. Here is an example:

1. Accidents, if fatal, if one or more persons is critically injured, or if someone of prominence is involved.

2. Major burglaries or series of burglaries which might be plaguing a community.

3. Major robberies, especially if someone is injured.

4. Larcenies involving large amounts of money or valuables.

5. Murders.

6. Gambling raids.

7. Jail breaks.

8. Major fires involving heavy damage, persons being burned out of their homes, landmarks destroyed, deaths or related injuries. Follow-up stories are included if clothing and fund drives or rebuilding is involved.

9. Suicides, but only if prominent persons are involved.

10. City council or county board meetings if the story is of general interest over a wide area.

11. Law suits, if prominent persons are involved or if large sums of money are mentioned.

12. Political news such as announcements of candidacy for major offices, changes in local political leadership, or squabbles within or between political parties.

13. Missing persons in cases where authorities are investigating.

14. Resignations and retirements, if out of the ordinary.

15. Speeches, if something hitherto unknown is disclosed, or it if involves controversy.

16. Weather, if something unusual occurs, or if violent weather or flooding occurs.

17. Strikes of any type.

18. Farm news in rural areas, stories involving county-wide meetings, crop reports, harvest information and, of course, farm and ranch accidents of a serious nature.

19. Feature stories with human interest (confirm that the editor is interested before you develop the story).

(These stories are not listed in order of importance.)

PUBLIC RELATIONS SOURCES

Newspapers and radio and television stations in large cities receive many news releases. Most are from public relations firms in the business of promoting the positive side of their clients. While many such releases contain news, rarely are the releases or handouts used in the form received. They are handled like normal news stories. The editor assigns a reporter to check the facts and write the story. The reporter handling such PR releases should never be content to use only the material contained in the releases.

NONLOCAL NEWS SOURCES

More than a century ago, soon after the arrival of the telegraph, newspapers began to organize cooperative press associations to gather and distribute nonlocal news. One of the earliest cooperatives was the Associated Press, founded by the New York morning papers in 1848 to collect foreign news from the latest issues of European newspapers arriving at East Coast seaports.

Today, the Associated Press and United Press International are the major press associations in the United States. The AP is incorporated as a membership cooperative with newspapers, radio and television stations, and networks sharing its services and costs. The United Press International, however, is a private corporation. Newspapers and radio and television stations buy the UPI news service.

Although AP and UPI appear to be different, their operations are similar. Both provide a variety of news wires to

Fig. 3-2. This Associated Press Photofax receiver has just printed a black-and-white sports photograph. The caption is visible to the left of the picture. Newspaper and television newsrooms make much use of such still photographs.

Fig. 3-3. This is a United Press International Unifax picture receiver. As the pictures are printed, the roller at the top of the receiver slowly gathers the photographs.

Fig. 3-4. This is Katy the computer, located in the Kansas City Bureau of the Associated Press. This model is a PDP-8 manufactured by the Digital Equipment Corp. It is capable of receiving 1320 words a minute in news copy or transmitting 2046 words per minute. News stories are coded, depending on their importance, and placed in the computer. It automatically channels the news stories to the correct news wires in the order desired.

newspapers and radio and television stations, including CATV operations that originate local news programs.

Radio and TV stations usually obtain the broadcast wire. It provides frequent summaries of world, national, and regional news plus weather information, sports, and features.

Newspapers usually have the "A" wire, the major wire for news. But instead of providing newspapers with hourly summaries of news, the major newspaper wires concentrate on providing groupings of stories twice daily; one for morning newspapers, one for evening newspapers.

The AP and UPI also provide secondary wires with regional news coverage, plus sports and business wires. Some large broadcast newsrooms use these wires to obtain more detailed information.

Most newspapers subscribe to either the AP or UPI still picture services. Using automatic picture printers, the AP Photofax (see Fig. 3-2) and UPI Unifax (see Fig. 3-3) machines receive black-and-white photographs with captions. These photos may relate to major news events or public figures, or contain feature material. Many television stations subscribe to the picture services. The TV operations employ artists to tint wirephoto pictures with color so they will be compatible when shown on color television.

United Press International provides an audio news service with regular news programs plus actuality reports—the sounds of persons in the news. The Associated Press does not operate such a national audio service, but they do have numerous regional audio exchanges established as cooperatives among member radio and television stations.

COMPUTERS, ELECTRONIC GADGETS AND NEWS

During the 1960s the major radio and television networks began to make extensive use of computers to tabulate results from elections. By the late 1960s, other uses were being found for computers and related electronic equipment.

Today, many newspapers have installed or are installing computerized systems to speed up the process of news preparation and the makeup of newspaper pages. The Associated Press and United Press International are also using computers to increase the speed of news dissemination

Fig. 3-5. All Associated Press news wires in the United States pass through the AP's Kansas City Bureau. It is, as one AP official said, the "neck of the hourglass" in the national AP news operation. The large bank of equipment shown above acts as the interface between computerization and the newspaper and broadcast news wire located in newspapers and radio and television stations.

Fig. 3-6. The unit in the center of this photo is a CRT/Hendrix 5200. It displays a video picture of the news story typed by the news writer. This CRT (for cathode-ray tube) unit is located in the Kansas City Associated Press Bureau.

to newspapers and radio and television stations. (See Figs. 3-4 and 3-5.) The Associated Press is using the CRT/Hendrix 5200, an electronic unit that displays a video picture of a news story. (See Fig. 3-6.) The CRT enables the news writer to type a news story on a video screen and edit the story electronically. When the story is ready for dissemination, the news writer simply pushes a button and the story is fed into the computer. There, depending upon the story's priority, it is either stored or transmitted immediately to newspapers or broadcast stations.

EXERCISES

1. Make arrangements to visit the newsrooms of your local newspapers and radio and television stations. Interview the editors and news directors. Take notes. Determine:
   (a) How many reporters each newsroom employs?
   (b) What nonlocal news sources does each newsroom use?
   (c) What methods of gathering local news are used?
   (d) How extensive are the news beats of each newsroom?
   (e) What qualifications do the editors and news directors demand when hiring reporters?

2. Using the information obtained on your visits to the newspaper, radio, and television newsrooms, write a report on how local news is gathered by the news media in your community.

Chapter 4

Preparation of News Copy

> Nothing is more practical than
> the "rules" for getting copy
> ready for the printer or the
> announcer.
>
> Mitchell V. Charnley

Every newsroom has its own procedures to follow in preparing news copy. Such rules are necessary to eliminate needless confusion. Sloppy copy can cause inaccuracy or delay in editing stories for the newspaper or may cause the broadcast newsman to goof on the air.

There are major differences in the preparation of copy for the newspaper and the broadcast newsroom. What follows are the generally accepted rules, first for newspapers, then for broadcast news copy.

PREPARATION OF NEWSPAPER COPY

1. Use 8½ x 11 in. newsprint. Type only on one side of the paper. Some newsrooms require writers to use copy books, each having two to five second sheets with carbon attached.

2. Do not type stories only in upper case. Use upper and lower cases.

3. Stories should be triple-spaced, never single-spaced. (Some newspapers prefer double-spaced copy.) Double or triple-spaced copy permits editing between the lines of typing.

4. The writer should type his name, a "slug line" identifying the nature of the news story, and the date on three lines in the upper left-hand corner of the first page. Example:

Jones	(writer's name)
Oil fire	("slug line")
Dec. 21	(date)

```
jones
oil fire
dec. 21




     Two men died today in the explosion of an oil storage

tank near Kansas City, Mo.   Firemen battled the blaze that

followed for three hours before bringing it under control.

Damage is estimated at more than $100,000.

     Police identify the dead men as William Allen Smith,

45, of Kansas City, Mo., and Elmer Davis, 56, of Independence,

Mo.  Both men were working near the storage tank when the

explosion occurred.

     The cause of the explosion is unknown.
```

Fig. 4-1. A correctly prepared typewritten newspaper story.

5. If the story runs more than one page, the word "more" must be placed at the bottom center of the first page. It should be circled by pencil. **All material not intended to be set into type is circled**.

6. The writer's last name, the "slug line," and the number of the succeeding page must be placed in the upper left-hand corner of all additional pages.

7. Begin typing your story about one-third the way down the first page. Leave one-inch margins at the left and right. Indent paragraph beginnings liberally for ease in copy editing.

8. Indicate the end of your story. Place one of the common end marks ("#" or "30" or "ENDIT") at the end of your story. Circle it. This tells the news desk there is no more copy to come.

9. When you have finished your story, read your copy over carefully. Make corrections or changes neatly with a pencil. (See Chapter 12.)

The importance of following newspaper copy preparation rules cannot be stressed enough. After the reporter completes a story, the copyreader reads and edits the material. Then it is sent to the print shop to be set in type.

By the very nature of the newspaper operation, copy preparation rules must be followed if the overall news dissemination process is to run smoothly. See Fig. 4-1 for an example of a correctly prepared typewritten newspaper story.

PREPARATION OF RADIO NEWS COPY

The preparation of radio news copy at the station level is usually the preparation of the on-air script. Therefore, careful attention must be paid to the following mechanics:

1. Use standard 8½ x 11 in. paper. (In cases where the actual news script is being prepared, a heavy bond paper is usually used in place of newsprint.

2. Type on one side of the paper only.

3. Do not type stories only in upper case. Use upper and lower case. (The AP and UPI broadcast news wires deliver news copy in all caps. This aids the speed of delivery. On-air newsmen, however, generally find that copy typed in lower and upper cases is easier to read than copy typed in all caps, provided the type is not too small.)

4. One story per page.

5. End each page of copy with a complete paragraph.

6. Never divide words, figures, or hyphenated phrases at the end of a line. The on-air newsman may have difficulty following the copy.

7. The writer should type his name, a "slug line" identifying the nature of the news story, and the date on three lines in the upper left-hand corner of the first page. Some radio newsrooms, however, prefer to have each story clocked-off at the end. Clocking-off a story indicates when the story was written, the date, and the initials of the writer. Example:

jj	(initials of writer)
4:23 p.m.	(time story was written)
10-4	(date)

```
┌─────────────────────────────────────────────┐
│                                             │
│  Station XXXX-TV              Page number _____  │
│                                             │
│  Story Title_____  Date_____  │
│                                             │
│  ═══════════════════════════════════════════  │
│  visual              │       audio            │
│                      │                        │
│                      │                        │
│                      │                        │
│                      │                        │
│                      │                        │
│                      │                        │
│                      │                        │
│                      │                        │
│                      │                        │
│                      │                        │
│                      │                        │
│                      │                        │
│                      │                        │
│                      │                        │
│                      │                        │
│                      │                        │
│                      │                        │
│                      │                        │
│                      │                        │
│                      │                        │
│                      │                        │
│                      │                        │
│                      │                        │
└─────────────────────────────────────────────┘
```

Fig. 4-2. The split-page form used in the preparation of television news copy.

In broadcast news writing the exact time a story is written is more critical than in newspaper copy.

PREPARATION OF TELEVISION NEWS COPY

Because television is a medium of visual and oral communication, the television news writer must consider both aspects in preparing news copy. Nearly all television news operations use the split-page form to prepare news stories that include visual material. Half a page is devoted to an outline of the visual material to be presented, and the remainder of the page contains the written narration.

The split-page form (see Fig. 4-2) enables the television director in the control room to easily follow both visual and oral requirements. Therefore, it is essential that the visual material correspond to the written material on each page. The mechanics of television news copy are summarized below:

1. Type only on one side of the split-page form.

2. Do not type stories only in upper case. Use upper and lower cases. (The writer may wish to use all caps, however, in outlining corresponding visual material in the left-hand column.)

3. End each page of copy with a complete sentence.

4. Never divide words, figures, or hyphenated phrases at the end of a line.

5. One story per page.

EXERCISE

1. On your visit to the local newspapers and radio and television stations (see the first exercise at the end of Chapter 3), ask to see how news copy is prepared. Determine what rules apply to the preparation of news copy at each operation you visit.

Chapter 5

News Writing Philosophy

> To write news in its perfection
> requires such a combination of
> qualities that a man completely
> fit for the task is not always to be
> found.
>
> Samuel Johnson

Many persons would have you believe that the act of writing consists only of arranging words in rows on paper. They assure you that anyone can write because, as Mark Twain once remarked, the words are all in the dictionary. But writing is not so simple, especially news writing. News writing is a complex art and a craft.

Words have meanings, most of them several meanings that vary according to the context or arrangement in which they are placed. The almost unlimited series of possible word combinations provide the real challenge to the writer. It is this challenge that, in part, makes news writing so fascinating a vocation, one which can never grow stale.

NEWS WRITING IS NONFICTION WRITING

The writer of fiction may decide what his story is going to be, who his characters are, and whether there will be a happy or sad ending. The news writer, however, does not have this choice. He must tell the story as it happened. He may not have a happy ending or even know how an event turned out when he is forced, by his deadline, to write the story.

Millions of people never read any fiction whatever, and millions more may read it only a few years out of their lifetime. But everybody writes nonfiction and everybody reads it. The news writer and his audience have one common bond—interest in nonfiction.

ACCURACY

Of all the complaints about news reporting today, inaccuracy is perhaps the one heard more often than any other. Let a newspaper or broadcast station report something that is untrue and the editor or news director may be verbally attacked from all sides. The public does not like to be fooled. They expect and demand the truth. When they are not given the truth, and learn it for themselves elsewhere, they begin to question the believability of the newspaper or broadcast station that reported the untruth. And, as an audience, they continue to question most, if not everything, the news organization reports.

In news writing, inaccuracy is usually caused by carelessness. Some newsrooms, even those in large cities, condone a certain amount of carelessness, but not too many. The better news operations demand and insist upon a high standard of accuracy. The old International News Service, now part of the United Press International, had a motto. It hung on most INS newsroom walls. It read: "Get it First, but FIRST get it RIGHT." This is good advice today.

SPEED

As the INS motto indicated, speed is important to news. The person who buys a newspaper or news magazine does so for the news. The sponsor of a radio or television news program pays to have his advertising announcements broadcast to an audience attracted by the news program. News is a business and the business is competitive.

The wire services that serve the media are competitive. Each wants to deliver the news ahead of his competitor. So do the various newspapers, radio and television networks, and individual stations that rely, to a great extent, upon the wire services for nonlocal news.

In such an atmosphere the news writer does not have the luxury of time. A novelist may work at his own pace, writing and rewriting until his product is polished. But the news writer does not have the time. He is under constant pressure to produce. (Fig. 5-1.)

While speed is important to both print and broadcast news writers, speed is perhaps more critical in broadcasting

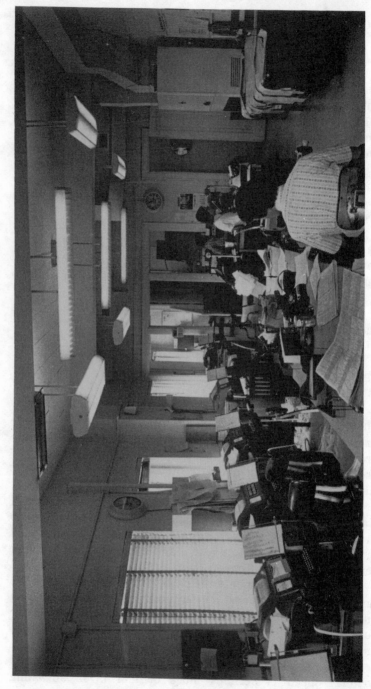

Fig. 5-1. This photo shows the United Press International regional bureau in Kansas City, Missouri.

because of the immediacy factor. Radio and television, including CATV, are fast. News deadlines in broadcast journalism are NOW. The element of immediacy in broadcasting forces the broadcast news writer to produce news copy at a more rapid pace than the newspaper or news magazine writer. But unlike the print journalist, who usually relates detailed accounts of news events, the broadcast newsman generally relates only brief stories, seldom in much detail.

CLARITY

Speed and accuracy mean very little in news reporting if the news is not clearly written. Clarity in news copy is essential if the reader or listener is to understand the story.

Clarity in news begins in the writer's mind. The writer first must understand the story. If not, how can he expect to communicate the story to his audience? And the news writer must ask himself, "What do these facts mean to my audience?" "What is the story?" "What is the news?" Once these questions are answered, the writer can begin to organize his material and write the story. (Fig. 5-2.)

The news writer must remember that the purpose of news writing is to communicate rapidly. Therefore, it is essential that the finished product be clear, precise, and to the point. Clarity is a must. Without clarity the news writer will fail to communicate the ideas and information of the story to his audience.

THE PAUL WHITE THEORY

Many years ago the late Paul White, CBS radio's first news director, wrote that broadcast news writers must do three things to make certain their news copy is clearly understood by listeners. White said the writer must **tell the listener what he is going to tell him...then tell him... then tell him what he has told him.** If this is done, said White, there is little chance the listener will miss the important elements of the story.

During the 1930s and early '40s, the belief was widespread that repetition in radio news writing guaranteed

Fig. 5-2. NBC News Correspondent David McClure Brinkley started his career as a newsman during high school. Brinkley worked as a reporter on several newspapers before joining United Press in 1942. Working for a wire service taught Brinkley the skill of expressing an idea in the fewest possible words yet with maximum impact. In 1943 Brinkley joined NBC News in Washington, D.C., as a news writer. (Courtesy NBC.)

clarity. But then the broadcast journalists' attitude toward repetition began to change. Today, repetition is frowned upon by many radio and television news writers. Clear and simple language and better organization of material has replaced the need for repetition.

STYLE

The word **style** has many definitions. It may be used to describe how a friend walks or talks. It may refer to the type of furniture in your neighbor's home, or it may concern a mode of living. But in journalism, style refers to writing.

The words **manner** and **style**, as they apply to journalism, are sometimes taken to mean the same thing. They are different. Manner refers to the differences in writing for one medium opposed to another, while style refers to how a writer writes.

News writing style depends upon the writer. His style, in part, is his personality, his skill with words, and the overall effectiveness of his final product. If a news writer uses the English language effectively in telling the story in a clear, concise, and correct form, his style probably is good.

Style in news writing may also refer to the rules of writing as established by a newspaper or a broadcast news director. Many newspapers and broadcast news operations have their own style books or style sheets. These contain uniform rules of grammar, spelling, syntax, abbreviations, capitalization, and so forth. They help to establish precision and consistency in all writing produced for the particular news operation. If such rules did not exist, there would be anarchy.

But any style book or style sheet is no substitute for thinking. The style manual does not do the news writer's job. It does not tell him how to write the lead or how to organize the story. The news writer must solve these problems on his own. They require much thought and work.

UNITY OF NEWSPAPER STYLE

In 1960, the Associated Press and the United Press International news services agreed to abide by one newspaper

Fig. 5-3. This is the first broadcast news style book written for any wire service. Phil Newsom, United Press radio news manager, wrote this 42-page book in 1943. It sold for 75 cents. Today it is a collector's item.

style book. They reached agreement on what is becoming an accepted newspaper style in many newsrooms. And the AP-UPI newspaper style book is regularly revised.

Although much of the AP-UPI style book has been reproduced in the back of this book, complete copies may be purchased from Associated Press, 50 Rockefeller Plaza, New York, 10020, or from United Press International, 220 East 42nd Street, New York, New York, 10017.

The AP and UPI also have their own broadcast news style books. Although similar, they are not identical. They reflect the different approaches taken by the two wire services in broadcast news writing. Copies of the AP and UPI broadcast news style books may also be obtained by writing to the addresses listed above. (See Fig. 5-3.)

THE NEW YORK TIMES STYLE BOOK

Perhaps the most respected style manual is that of **The New York Times**. Edited and revised by Lewis Jordan, **The New York Times Style Book** sets rules of writing for **The New York Times**. The book is published by McGraw-Hill Book Company in New York City.

Lewis Jordan points out in the foreword that **The New York Times Style Book** "cannot provide the answer to every question of style that may come up. Sometimes the answer may be reached by analogy. The rule should encourage thinking, not discourage it. Ideally, a single rule might suffice: 'The rule of common sense will prevail at all times.' "

HEMINGWAY AND THE KANSAS CITY STAR

The influence of a good style book or style sheet upon a news writer is reflected in Ernest Hemingway's experience as a young reporter on **The Kansas City Star** between October 1917 and April 1918. In 1940, more than 20 years after leaving the **Star**, Hemingway was asked what rules had most helped him in his writing. He replied that it was the first paragraph of the **Star**'s style sheet.

"Those were the best rules I ever learned for the business of writing. I've never forgotten them. No man with any talent,

The Star

(Sep

Rules 1 to 16, inc.

Use short sentences. Use short first paragraphs. Use vigorous English. Be positive, not negative.

The style of local communications is *To The Star:* in italics; out-of-town communications in this form: Salina, Kas.—*To The Star:*

Never use old slang. Such words as *stunt, cut out, got his goat, come across, sit up and take notice, put one over,* have no place after their use becomes common. Slang to be enjoyable must be fresh.

Use *Kas.,* not *Kan.* or *Kans.,* as an abbreviation for Kansas; use *Ok.,* not *Okla.,* for Oklahoma; *Col.,* not *Colo.,* for Colorado; *Cal.,* not *Calif.,* for California.

Watch your sequence of tenses. "He said he knew the truth," not "He said he *knows* the truth." "The community was amazed to hear that Charles Wakefield *was a thief,*" not "*was amazed to hear that Charles Wakefield is a thief.*"

...sons are sleepi... in other cases. ...an accident." ...done for anyth...

"He *suffered*... not "*he broke*... didn't break th... leg, not his leg... man has two le...

"The work b... begun."

He *was* grad... "*he graduated*...

Say Mary w... —not "*in comp*...

"Honor the... Karnes," not... after his death...

Say "John... comma betwee...

"Mr. Roosevel... lieve, would s... believe, would.'

"Mr. Roosevel... believe, the p...

Fig. 5-4. This photograph shows a portion of **The Kansas City Star** style sheet as it appeared in the early 1920s, not long after Ernest Hemingway spent several months as a reporter on the **Star**. Hemingway said the first three lines of the style sheet was the best writing advice he had ever received.

who feels and writes truly about the thing he is trying to say, can fail to write well if he abides with them," said Hemingway. The first paragraph of the **Star's** style sheet reads today as it did in 1917:

> **Use short sentences. Use short first paragraphs.**
>
> **Use vigorous English. Be positive, not negative.**

This is the best advice any news writer can follow (see Fig. 5-4).

EXERCISES

1. Obtain an 8½ x 11 in. piece of paper. Rule off four columns up and down on the paper. At the top of the first column, left side, write the word **stories**. At the top of the second column from the left side write the word **accuracy**. At the top of the third column from the left write the word **clarity**. At the top of the fourth column write the word **style**. Now obtain two or more newspapers of the same day of publication in your area. Carefully read the local and area news stories reported by the newspapers. When you find the same story reported by two or more newspapers, clip those stories. Compare them for accuracy, clarity, and style. Write your comments in the respective columns on the piece of paper. Note the differences in the writing and the reporting of identical stories.

2. Using a tape recorder, record two or more local radio news programs aired during the early afternoon. Compare the radio station's local and area news coverage to that of the evening newspapers.

Chapter 6

The Language of News

Plain talk is the language of the people.
Rudolf Flesch

The dictionary defines a word as "a sound or a combination of sounds which, through conventional association with some fixed meaning, communicates an idea." Words, then, are sounds to which meanings have been given. In news writing, as in any kind of writing, sound and meaning are two elements with which the writer must deal.

Most authorities estimate that the English language contains more than 600,000 words. However, perhaps only 10,000 of these are fully understood by the average reader or listener. Thus, if the news writer is to communicate, he must use words his audience will understand.

THE SYNTAX OF THE NEWS SENTENCE

Syntax is defined as the way in which words are put together to form phrases and sentences. The syntax or order of the normal news sentence, whether for print or broadcast, is (1) subject, (2) the finite verb, (3) the indirect object, or (4) the direct object. A news writer should deviate from this order when he wishes to emphasize a sentence element other than the subject.

The emphatic or accentuated parts of a sentence are the beginning and the end. Usually, in a long sentence the end is accentuated more than the beginning because the thought builds up a climax. But news stories are best told in short sentences containing no more than one thought. Placing two or more ideas in one sentence may confuse the reader or listener. And putting too many thoughts in a sentence also makes the news writer's job more difficult.

A writer also may confuse the reader or listener by putting parallel thoughts in constructions that are not grammatically parallel. News writers should follow the rule that "like meanings should be put in like constructions."

A common violation of parallelism is to use an infinitive and a gerund (a word used as a noun but conveying the meaning of the verb) in a parallel construction. Example:

Bad: "One of the bills was approved but rejections were voted on the others."
Good: "One of the bills was approved but the others were rejected."

THE NEWS PARAGRAPH

In books and magazines, a paragraph is a unit of thought. This is not always the case in newspaper and broadcast news copy. The traditional paragraph of the English language does not, as a rule, exist in news writing. Newspaper paragraphs are used primarily as a typographical device for maintaining attention, while in broadcast news copy they provide the on-air reporter with a spot to pause for a breath or the opportunity to end a news story. The broadcast listener, of course, never sees the paragraphs in broadcast copy.

WORD SELECTION HELPS CLARITY

The words selected by the news writer to tell the story determine, in part, the clarity of the news story. Consider the words used in the following front page story from the **New York Daily Tribune**, September 21, 1849:

> Quite a respectable congregation collected last evening, at the established hour of "early candlelight," in front of the City Hall, to listen to a very rational and edifying discourse on the evils of intemperance, by a sallow and pious-looking individual, who seemed to speak with great feeling and sincerity. The congregation was as orderly and attentive as a church; and we only hope that a majority of its members escaped the innumerable grogshops and drinking-cellars in the vicinity, on their way home. It is really almost an impossibility for a man with a liquorish tooth in his head, to go from the Park in any direction without tumbling into some of them.

The language of this story is somewhat formal, typical of the literary style of news writing in the 1840s. The writer injected subtle opinion and used more words than necessary to tell the story. A modern version of the story, without the writer's opinion and attempt at humor, might read:

> An unidentified man spoke on the evils of
> liquor in front of city hall last night.
> He attracted a large audience.

This rewrite shows the more conversational approach of news writing today.

During the past 50 years, radio and television's conversational or oral style of news writing and presentation has greatly influenced newspaper style. In 1960, Carl E. Lindstrom, who worked for many years on the Hartford, Connecticut, **Times**, observed in his book, **The Fading American Newspaper**: "We are approaching the end of an era. Each of the periods of our language has lasted four hundred to six hundred years: Old English, roughly from 500 to 1100; Middle English from 1100 to 1500. Modern English has now had its four hundred years and a little more. Maybe time is up. Evidence could be cited in the development of radio and television, with their oral journalism, and the growing emphasis upon visual aids. The language is rapidly being oralized."

A noticeable change in the language of some newspaper writing occurred during World War II as radio news matured. Many newspaper writers began to use a more conversational style. After the war, in 1947, the editors of the now defunct International News Service wrote in the revised edition of their **INS Radio News Manual**:

"It was recognized that most news writing in newspaper offices and radio stations, too, was suffering an 1890 hangover. There were too many inversions, dangling participles, modifying phrases, and attributive clauses. There were too many high-sounding words and trick phrases. The average news story was so involved and complicated that it tripped the reader's eye, to say nothing of his tongue.

"The editors of INS went into the whole subject. Surveys were made, tests conducted, and words and phrases were analyzed. The editors came to one important conclusion: that there is a close relationship between writing for the eye and the ear. An improvement for one is also an improvement for the other. Simplicity is the keynote.

"Breaking up a long, involved 'lead' into direct, concise sentences benefits the newspaper reader as well as the radio listener. A clumsy dependent clause is just as unnatural to the eye as to the ear." INS reseachers also made careful notes of everyday conversations. They found that the average man tells a story in concise, simple sentences.

From all this research, the editors drew up rules for achieving a new, direct, streamlined style which would appeal to both the eye and the ear. INS writers began 'talking out' their stories—reading them aloud as they wrote them. Gradually and without fanfare, the INS news wire was completely restyled."

Three years later Dr. Rudolf Flesch of New York University completed a writing study for the Associated Press. Flesch recommended that the AP reduce its habitually long sentences (they averaged about 27 words) to 19 words. Flesch told the AP:

" 'Reading ease' is measured by the average length of words and sentences—the shorter, the easier to read. My studies have shown that an average word length of 1.5 syllables and an average sentence length of 19 words is a good standard for newspaper material.

" 'Human interest' is measured by the percentage of 'personal words' and 'personal sentences.' These include names, pronouns, and certain other words referring to people, and direct quotes, questions, 'you' sentences, and other sentences indirectly addressed to another person. The more of these 'personal' elements, the more interesting for the average reader. My studies have shown that 6 percent 'personal words' and 12 percent 'personal sentences' make a good standard for news writing." wrote Flesch.

At about the same time, Robert Gunning, director of Readable News Reports, of Columbus, Ohio, conducted a study for United Press. Gunning concluded, among other things, that the reader begins to have difficulty when the average number of words per sentence exceeds 20. Gunning pointed out that **Time**, the news magazine, averaged 16 to 18 words per sentence while **Readers Digest** sentences averaged 18. Gunning noted that their popularity may depend more on the way they were written than on what they contain. **Atlantic Monthly**, in contrast, averaged 24 words per sentence and appealed to so-called "high brows."

The formula writing recommendations of Flesch, Gunning, and others have been criticized for wasting the writer's time and skill and killing writer creativeness. But they have caused writers to think more of their writing. Interestingly, about 12 years after the Flesch report was issued, the Associated Press announced that the ease-of-reading level of its prose had reached the point it sought. And in 1964 an analysis of AP copy showed its average sentence length to be 18.7.

Today, changes in news writing continue. Compare the writing in any metropolitan newspaper today to that of the same newspaper ten years ago. The change will be obvious. An example of good contemporary news writing, with a touch of human interest, is the following front-page story by Ted Thackrey, Jr., reprinted from the **Los Angeles Times**:

> It will begin quietly next Sunday afternoon, in Iceland.
>
> Promptly at 2 p.m. (Icelandic time), a Russian and an American will sit down to play a game of chess in a small auditorium at Reykjavik.
>
> During the five hours that follow they probably will not exchange a dozen words. Nor will the audience. To a casual observer, it all might seem about as exciting and dramatic as a visit to a mausoleum.
>
> But there will be no casual observers.
>
> For this will be the first in a series of 24 games to decide the chess championship of the world — and this confrontation has drawn more worldwide interest than any other event of its kind in history.
>
> Indeed, in terms of tension and suspense this year's match would compare favorably with an Alfred Hitchcock movie. The script thus far reads like something adapted from the words of Graham Greene.
>
> ### Spassky vs Fischer
>
> And the characters are pure Dostoevsky:
> The present champion, Boris Vasilyevich Spassky, a broad-shouldered bear who knows he must maintain the dominance that Russians have held in world chess since 1937, or face the consequences.
>
> The challenger, Robert James (Bobby) Fischer, gangling, Chicago-born "enfant terrible of the chess world" who has called himself the "unofficial world champion" for nearly a decade and who now must prove his claim.

The winner's end of the purse is $100,000 — and that alone could be a fair indicator of the difference between the championship matches of 1972 and those of the past.

The remainder of this story is just as conversational as that which you have read. It not only is good newspaper copy, it is good broadcast copy. It is clear writing.

UPI'S ADVICE

Clarity in news writing depends, in part, on the simplicity of the words used. The broadcast editors of United Press International use the following comparison to show their staff writers the difference between good and bad broadcast news writing:

Bad

(Sacramento) —— Fiscal watchdogs on the legislature's efficiency committee said today they will continue to probe the disclosure that the state's taxpayers will have no choice but to assume responsibility for the 93-million dollar freeway bonds despite a ruling by the attorney general's office to the contrary.

Good

(Sacramento) —— Lawmakers who watch the way California spends its money say they're continuing to study the freeway bond dispute. The bonds total 93-million dollars...and the question is whether California taxpayers might have to pay for them. The attorney general has ruled they will not...but financial advisors say he is wrong...that the taxpayers will have to pay for the bonds. Today...the legislature's efficiency committee announced it will continue to investigate just who must pay for the freeway bonds.

UPI also provides its broadcast news writers with a list of simple words that they feel will help to paint a better word picture when writing for the ear. The list includes:

—HURRY or just plain GO, not always RUSH.
—SEND something, don't always TRANSMIT or DISPATCH.
—CALL a person, don't SUMMON him.
—BUY something, rather than PURCHASE it.
—LEAVE a place, not just DEPART or EVACUATE.
—ACT, don't always TAKE ACTION.

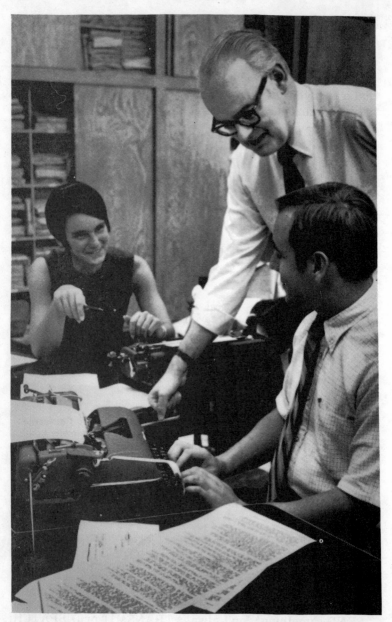

Fig. 6-1. Three broadcast news writers in the Los Angeles Associated Press office. Cal Werner (center), broadcast supervisor for California and Nevada, goes over copy with day broadcast supervisor Rachel Eberle and broadcast writer Lee Margulies. The broadcast control bureau at Los Angeles has more than seven staff members. (Courtesy AP)

—TRY, instead of ATTEMPT.

—ARREST, not always TAKE INTO CUSTODY.

—SHOW, rather than DISPLAY or EXHIBIT.

—GET, don't always OBTAIN.

—DOCTOR, not always PHYSICIAN.

—BREAK, instead of always FRACTURE.

AN NBC NEWS WRITING MEMO

If broadcast journalism students would have the opportunity to read internal news writing memos that shuffle from desk to desk in the large network newsrooms, they would learn more about the problems of writing. Of all the news writing memos that this writer read during seven years in network news, perhaps the best one was written by Jim Holton of NBC News in New York, late in 1966. The memo contains examples of bad writing on NBC Radio's "News on the Hour" programs. The memo, in part reads:

The quality of the writing on radio's News on the Hour programs has slumped. It must be improved. A study of Hourlies scripts from most programs of two days last week uncovered disheartening evidence of that decline. Attached are some of the more glaring examples, ranging from careless use of the language to outright inaccuracy. These examples came from scripts written by nearly as many correspondents as there are items. With very few exceptions each correspondent should recognize some of his own faulty prose:

CARELESS, CONTRIVED, INACCURATE WRITING (all in one 5-minute show)

"Nothing unexpected...but Red China has said 'nothing doing' to Canada's plan to seat Peking at the United Nations...

"As Americans become mobile on a holiday... the expected happens.

"Police in Los Angeles are telling the story of a sniper apparently shooting to kill. They say he wounded two people and terrorized a section of town early today...but there were no deaths.

81

"A powerful voice raised on birth control: 85 world **religious** leaders, including a **number of Nobel prize winners.....**"

IMPROPER USE OF THE PRONOUN

"Jordanian Security forces have clashed with demonstrators demanding the ouster of King Hussein. **They** accuse Hussein of being too easy on Israel....."

INTERNATIONAL DATELINE CONFUSION

(On a morning program the day after Thanksgiving) "Thanksgiving day found U.S. planes engaged in major attacks aginst the enemy..." (THE CURRENT WAR REPORTS THAT MORNING COVERED ACTION DURING THE DAY AFTER THANKSGIVING DAY, SAIGON TIME, DURING THANKSGIVING NIGHT, U.S. TIME.)

BAD WRITING

"...But sources say he found the Russian attitude unyielding on the issue that the United States immediately stop bombing North Vietnam and withdraw from the south before receiving concessions from the other side."

INACCURACY

"Three persons were killed and all train service halted **at New York's** Grand Central Terminal tonight when an automobile crashed through an overpass and plunged to the tracks." (THE CRASH OCCURRED SOME 130 BLOCKS NORTH OF THE TERMINAL.)

INCONSEQUENTIAL TIME WASTERS

"A U.S. Public Health Service report says American families least able to pay for necessary surgical operations are also the least likely to have their operations paid through insurance. The survey says that less than 34 percent of families earning under two thousand dollars a year had their surgical costs covered by insurance. For families earning more than 7 thousand a year, 81 percent of surgical costs were paid through insurance."

TIPPING THE SPOT

"The situation in the Jerusalem area of Jordan is growing worse. Troops of the Jordan Arab Legion drove through the streets of Ramallah, eight miles north of Jerusalem today, firing in the air above demonstrators. The tension results from dissatisfaction among Palestinian Arabs in Jordan because of what they consider King Hussein's moderation toward Israel. Palestinian Arabs, many of whom come from what is now Israel, hate the Israelis, want arms to fight them. We'll have a report." (WHY BOTHER NOW?)

TENSE

"....at least 48,000 enemy troops **have** moved from the North into South Vietnam between January first and September 30th."

MISSING DETAILS

"An allied road convoy has been ambushed in the central highlands. Four Americans were among the 18 victims....."

TRITE PHRASES

"...with the breakaway colony of Rhodesia..."

NUMBER

"Britain has warned Rhodesia that if **they** continue to reject..."

CARELESS PHRASING

"...a DC-3 airliner of Aden Airways crashed in the Mid-East with all 28 persons aboard killed."

POOR ORGANIZATION

Lead item: "It's been fairly quiet in Vietnam today—except for an ambush of a U.S. convoy and a mass kidnaping. Twenty people are believed to have been killed in the ambush, including seven Americans. They were workers of a U.S.

communications company." Final item: "On that mass kidnaping in South Vietnam today, it happened deep in the Mekong Delta..." (etc. for 30 seconds).

EXERCISES

1. Select a lengthy news story from a local or area newspaper. Carefully read the story. On separate paper list those words containing four or more syllables. Using a dictionary, list synonyms for the long words. Select only synonyms with fewer syllables than in the original words. Determine if the writer of the news story could have used simpler words to tell the story.

2. Using the newspaper story selected for exercise one (above), determine if the writer has expressed more than one thought in any of his sentences. If so, write the thoughts in separate sentences, keeping one thought per sentence. Try to improve the clarity of the story.

Chapter 7

Structuring a News Story

A love for words and their ways is not enough. You must also find pleasure in patterns, delight in design; you must acquire a love of longer units of expression—the paragraph, the sentence, and the whole composition.

Walter S. Campbell

News writing, as we know it today, is about 130 years old. It has grown up naturally out of the ever-changing character of the American newspaper. It has evolved. It continues to change.

CHRONOLOGICAL FORM

In the 1840s and '50s, American news writers followed no particular pattern in organizing their stories. Most stories were rambling. They were organized and written in chronological order much like British news stories. They were loosely presented in the narrative form of an English theme (Fig. 7-1). The first paragraph of William Howard Russell's account of the charge of the Light Brigade during the Crimean War, published by the London **Times**, November 13, 1854, is an example of the British style that was adapted in the United States:

HEIGHTS BEFORE SEBASTOPOL, OCTOBER 25—If the exhibition of the most brillant valor, of the excess of courage, and of a daring which would have reflected luster on the best days of chivalry can afford full consolation for the disaster of today, we can have no reason to regret the melancholy loss which we sustained in a contest with a savage and barbarian enemy.

By today's news writing standards, Russell's story is not acceptable. The beginning is unclear. It does not summarize the important elements of the story. The reader is not told who, what, when, where, and why at the beginning.

85

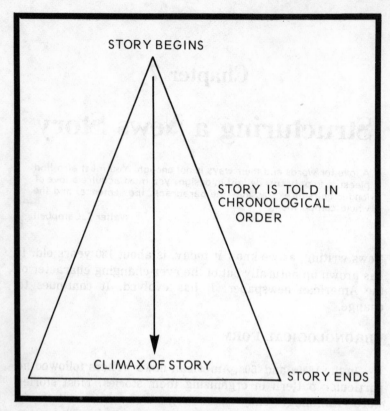

STORY BEGINS

STORY IS TOLD IN
CHRONOLOGICAL
ORDER

CLIMAX OF STORY

STORY ENDS

Fig. 7-1. The chronological story form used until the 1860s by news writers in the United States. It was borrowed from British journalists.

If William Howard Russell had, in the beginning, included the facts that "some 607 men of an English light cavalry brigade, fighting in the Crimean War, charged a heavily protected Russian artillery post at Balaklava, eight miles from Sebastopol, and only 198 British soldiers survived," the modern-day reader would find the story more acceptable. The story would have been in the form most common today. But it was not. Russell wrote the story much like other journalists of his day. This story form was used in the United States until the 1860s.

DOUBLE-ENDED FORM

During the Civil War, telegraph service was not too reliable. To make certain the who, what, when, where, and why of a story reached the newspapers from the battefields, reporters began sending brief summaries of their stories before having the detailed versions telegraphed. The reporters' thinking was that the summary would reach the newspaper even though the detailed version might be delayed. This form is know as the double-ended story (Fig. 7-2).

INVERTED PYRAMID

By the 1870s the double-ended form was gradually being replaced by what became known as the inverted pyramid form (Fig. 7-3). This story form was developed to suit the needs of the growing Associated Press.

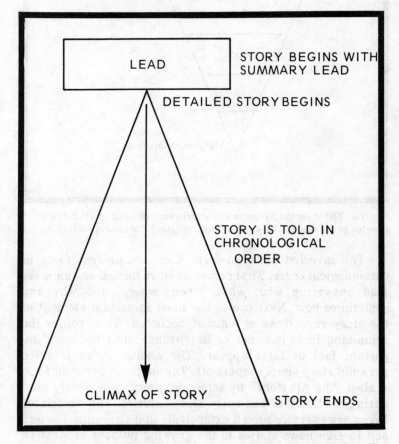

Fig. 7-2. The double-ended story form that developed during the American Civil War.

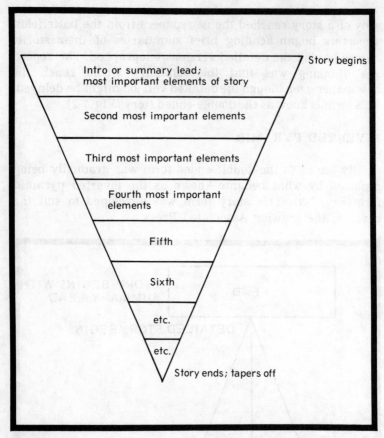

Fig. 7-3. The inverted pyramid story form was developed after the Civil War for press association stories. This form facilitates easy editing.

The inverted pyramid form does not present facts in chronological order. First comes an introduction or **summary lead** answering who, what, when, where, and why and sometimes how. Next comes the most important element of the story regardless of when it occurred. Then comes the remaining facts in order of importance until the least important fact or facts appear. The ending of an inverted pyramid story simply tapers off. The inverted pyramid form (called "the AP story" by some oldtimers) was widely used during the late 19th and early 20th centuries. The Associated Press news service used it extensively in distributing Eastern and foreign news stories to the growing number of Western newspapers whose editors had different story length needs.

The inverted pyramid form facilitates easy editing. An editor in Chicago might want to run the entire 900-word AP story detailing an Eastern train wreck, but an editor in Denver might decide the same story is worth only 200 words. The story, written in the inverted pyramid form, can easily be cut at the end of any paragraph after the summary lead. The important elements of the story remain regardless of where the story is cut.

Here is an example of an inverted pyramid story that appeared in the **New York Times** May 15, 1948:

Summary Lead

WASHINGTON, May 14 - President Truman asserted tonight that there would be a Democrat in the White House during the next four years and that he would be the man. He made the statement to a cheering audience of 1,000 young Democrats at their meeting here.

Body containing details

The President's speech was a fighting one in the new Truman manner. He spoke extemporaneously, resorting to whimsy and irony and using forceful gestures of his arms to underscore his points.

Mr. Truman accused the Republican party of stealing Democratic platform planks. "You know," he said, "it has been their habit since 1936 of taking a few planks out of the old Democratic platforms and building a platform and then saying, "Me, too."

"What have the Republicans done in the last fifteen and a half years?" Mr. Truman asked, then said:

"They have been obstructionists. They spent most of their time while I was in the Senate—and I was there ten years—in obstructing progressive legislation that was for the welfare of the common man, and throwing bricks and mud at the greatest President that ever sat in the White House."

Mr. Truman was interrupted by applause at this obvious allusion to President Roosevelt.

Although there are several more paragraphs to this story, the six paragraphs presented are sufficient to show the inverted pyramid form.

Fig. 7-4. ABC News Correspondent Howard K. Smith as he appeared in the middle 1960s. Notice the extensive research library to his right.

The structure of a broadcast news story often follows the inverted pyramid form. The main difference in broadcast and print stories is that radio and television stories are shorter. Consider the organization of the following Associated Press broadcast wire story:

Timely Lead

(St. Louis) - The hijacked American Airlines jetliner has returned to Lambert Airport tonight with the hijacker and 21 hostages still on board. The plane was being refueled shortly after landing.

The plane touched down shortly before 9:30 P.M.

Story Body

A radio operator at the airport who monitored the captain's calls from the hijacked plane says the hijacker plans to keep one passenger hostage on the flight and get a new crew for the plane.

Details

The radio operator—Mike McNeary of Midcoast Aviation Service—says the plane's captain indicated the hijacker wants to head toward Toronto, Canada, when he leaves here, and then fly to Kennedy Airport in New York.

More details

McNeary also said the hijacker sat in the rear of the passenger compartment throughout the return trip from the Fort Worth, Texas, area tonight. He said the hijacker threatened to kill a stewardess if his orders were not carried out.

The pilot of the hijacked jetliner described the hijacker as about five-feet-eleven, 170 pounds and about 25-years-old. He is also reportedly wearing a dark brown wig, brown suit, gold tie, and surgical gloves.

As shown, there are two main parts to an inverted pyramid story: the **lead** and the **body**. They will be discussed at some length in the chapters that follow.

EXERCISES

1. Obtain a recent copy of your local newspaper. Select ten news stories. Analyze each story. Determine what structure the writer used. Is it the inverted pyramid form? If not, what technique did the writer use to outline his story?

2. Using the ten news stories above, carefully read each story for clarity. On a note pad write those sentences or paragraphs that appear to be awkward or unclear. Rewrite the sentences that appear faulty. Try to improve the clarity of each sentence or paragraph.

3. Select a news story in your local newspaper. On a separate sheet of paper list the who, what, when, where, why, and how of the story. Next outline the news story without referring to the original story. Use only your notes. Now write the story. When it is finshed, analyze it. Look at the paragraphs (are they too short or too long?). Look at your sentences (do they have emphatic openings? Are they too long?). Look at your verbs (are they strong simple verbs?). Finally, using a pencil, see how many words can be cut or changed in your story to further improve the clarity.

Chapter 8

The Lead

There is nothing like a good beginning for a story.
Journalism stresses it.
Writers strive for it.
Editors demand it.

John Hohenberg

The news story lead, sometimes called the intro or summary lead, serves to summarize the story by answering the questions who, what, when, where, and often why and how. The lead acts as a signboard that reads: "Hey, look here." It attracts readers and listeners.

Leads vary in structure, length, and organization. A lead may begin with the subject, a phrase, or a clause. It depends on the nature of the story and the writer's skill. Read the following lead:

Frank W. Johnson, 5298 South Woodlawn Street, Jonesburg, a service station attendant, was robbed of $25 and a watch last night by two intoxicated robbers who accosted him as he was working on an auto at the service station where he works at 2429 South Brinkman Avenue.

While the above lead includes the who, what, when, and where of the story, it is wordy. It is cumbersome. It contains too much detail. It is what professionals call an overloaded lead.

For many years, one-sentence summary leads were considered standard in news writing. When radio began broadcasting news in the 1920s, however, the spoken word began to influence newspaper writing. Gradually, the long summary lead, like the example above, started to disappear. Today, such leads have shorter sentences and are more conversational. Brevity is stressed with the who, what, when, where, and why distributed through two or three sentences instead of one sentence. Read a newspaper rewrite of the robbery story:

> A Jonesburg man was robbed of $25 and a watch last night.
> Frank W. Johnson, a service station attendant, was repairing an auto in the service station where he works at 2429 South Brinkman Avenue when two intoxicated men accosted him.
> Johnson lives at 5298 South Woodlawn Street.

The readability has been improved. This version is more conversational than the first. The news writer has drawn the reader or listener into the story by not providing all of the facts in the lead sentence. Yet this story can be improved. On separate paper rewrite this story as many different ways as possible. Attempt to improve the lead.

LEADS VARY

No two leads are alike. As any professional journalist knows, no two writers will write a lead in the same style. Compare the following newspaper stories. the first was written by an Associated Press writer, the second by a United Press International writer:

> WASHINGTON (AP) - The Democratic Convention credentials committee voted Friday to unseat Chicago Mayor Richard J. Daley and 58 other uncommitted Illinois delegates to the national convention.
> The committee's action was a victory for Sen. George McGovern, who is expected to get at least 41 of the 59 delegates if the ruling is upheld by the convention in Miami Beach July 10.
> But like the credentials committee vote Thursday, stripping McGovern of more than half of the 271 California delegates, the Illinois seating fight further widened the split in the convention between the McGovern forces and those opposing him.

> WASHINGTON (UPI) The Democratic Convention's credentials committee dropped the other shoe Friday night with a vote denying delegate seats to Chicago Mayor Richard J. Daley and 58 of his allies.
> The action intensified the battle for those seats as well as a block of California delegates.
> The committee voted 71 to 61 to unseat the 59 uncommitted Illinois delegates captained by the taciturn mayor.

The Daley forces vowed to carry the fight to the convention floor and to a federal courtroom.

The victors were an insurgent group led by an anti-Daley Chicago alderman and the Rev. Jesse Jackson, a Black civil rights leader. They challenged the Daley bloc as unrepresentative of Blacks, young people, and women.

But another victor, too, was Sen. George McGovern, who is expected to gain at least 41 delegate votes because of the Daley delegation's defeat.

The UPI version is written with more color and action than the AP version. Does it detract from the facts of the story? Which version do you like best?

On separate paper list what you feel are the good points and the bad points of each version. Study the sentence construction, especially the placement of subject and the verbs used. Determine why you feel one version is better than the other. Now let us examine two versions of a **broadcast** news story. At about the same hour, shortly before noon on June 26, 1972, the AP and UPI broadcast wires carried summary stories on tropical storm Agnes:

AP Broadcast Version

RAVAGING FLOOD WATERS HAVE BEGUN TO RECEDE AT RICHMOND, VIRGINIA, AND IN SOME OTHER AREAS OF THE NORTHEAST. FIVE STATES HAVE BEEN DECLARED FEDERAL DISASTER AREAS. WESTERN PENNSYLVANIA WAS THE HARDEST HIT BY FLOODING TOUCHED OFF BY TROPICAL STORM AGNES. THOUSANDS OF PEOPLE HAVE BEEN FORCED FROM THEIR HOMES, NOT ONLY IN PENNSYLVANIA BUT IN SOME OTHER STATES. AT LEAST 81 LIVES HAVE BEEN LOST FROM FLORIDA TO NEW YORK, 31 OF THEM IN PENNSYLVANIA.

OFFICIALS ARE CALLING THE STORM ONE OF THE MOST DESTRUCTIVE IN HISTORY ALONG THE EASTERN SEABOARD.

AT LAST REPORT FROM THE WEATHER BUREAU THE REMAINS OF AGNES IS DRIFTING SLOWLY EASTWARD ACROSS NEW YORK. MANY RIVERS AND STREAMS THAT HAVE NOT ALREADY REACHED THEIR CREST ARE EXPECTED TO DO SO TODAY OR TONIGHT. BUT IT SAYS IT'LL BE SEVERAL DAYS BEFORE THE OHIO RIVER CRESTS DOWNSTREAM FROM PITTSBURGH. THE SUSQUEHANNA RIVER IN PENNSYLVANIA IS EXPECTED TO CREST 17 FEET ABOVE FLOOD STAGE TONIGHT AT HARRISBURG.

THE DEATH TOLL FROM TROPICAL STORM AGNES—
REMNANTS FROM THE HOWLER CONTINUE TO DELUGE
THE NORTHEASTERN U-S—IS NUDGING THE 100 MARK.
OFFICIALS NOW SAY 95 PERSONS ARE KNOWN DEAD...-
DAMAGE EXCEEDING ONE BILLION DOLLARS...MORE
THAN 250 THOUSAND PERSONS EVACUATED FROM THEIR
HOMES AND FIVE STATES DECLARED DISASTER AREAS.

THE HARDEST HIT AREA EXTENDS FROM THE
CAROLINAS TO NEW YORK, WITH PENNSYLVANIA SUF-
FERING THE MOST. FORTY PERSONS WERE KILLED...-
WHOLE CITIES EVACUATED BECAUSE OF RAMPAGING
FLOOD WATERS. THE STATE CAPITAL OF HARRISBURG
WAS INUNDATED.

Repeat the process of evaluation used for the newspaper examples. Which broadcast version do you like? Why? Remember these stories were written to be read aloud. Read them aloud. Listen to the sound of the words and phrases. Do they please the ear? Can you improve them?

The examples in this chapter have thus far represented straight news reporting. Now let us consider other techniques used to write leads.

THE ANECDOTAL LEAD

Magazines, including newspaper Sunday supplements, make frequent use of anecdotal leads. An anecdote—a short account of some interesting or humorous incident—attracts attention. An example is the following Associated Press story:

LONDON (AP) - For eight years Harry Hyams made millions by doing nothing.

He pioneered the idea that landlords can earn greater profits by keeping offices empty. It is perfectly legal. Hyams built up the biggest empire of empty office blocks in Britain.

The joke, which politicians called a national scandal, ended Monday night.

The British government declared war on empty office blocks in a new policy aimed primarily at Hyams and his property company, Oldham Estate, Ltd.

Environment Minister Peter Walker told a cheering House of Commons he would order new taxes or consider compulsory rentals unless the offices are rented in the next few months.

Hyams' company refused comment. But it was forced to rethink the policy on its four London office buildings including the most famous one, Centre Point, a 33-floor prestige block empty since it was finished eight years ago.

Centre stands at one end of Oxford St., London's department store row, occupied only by security guards and their dogs. It has been dubbed "the most expensive dog kennel in Britain."

When it was built, Centre Point Office space could have commanded rents of $11.20 a square foot for leases of 15 years. Today the same space would rent out for $18.40 a square foot.

Because of the acute shortage of office space in central London, the potential rental income of Centre Point kept skyrocketing as long as the building stayed empty. So did the shares of the property company in which Hyams is the main stockholder. That is how he made his money.

Another **Los Angeles Times** writer made good use of a short anecdotal lead when he or she wrote:

Deborah Ganz strapped on a gun and started work Tuesday as the first woman undercover inspector in the Internal Revenue Service.

She will be checking out IRS employees and people who try to bribe them.

The IRS has not hired women previously because the job was considered too dangerous.

But Miss Ganz is 24, healthy, and is an experienced IRS revenue collector.

THE PERSONAL LEAD

The personal approach often makes an otherwise dull story interesting. The news writer, however, must be careful not to over emphasize the personal lead. William J. Coughlin of the **Los Angeles Times** used a personal lead effectively in the following story:

HANNAOUIYE, Lebanon - If this mountain village within a few miles of the southern border of Israel is typical, relations between the Lebanese army and the Palestinian commandos camped near the border are good despite reports to the contrary.

The guerrillas moved freely and openly through army check-points in the region Tuesday. There was as yet no sign of withdrawal by the commandos, although negotiations by the government to induce them to leave continued in Beirut.

Another example is Morris David Rosenberg's personal lead in a story published by **The Washington Post**:

A trip to the Library of Congress these days will show you graphically how far the tourist has come (gone?) in the past 100 years. Perhaps too far, was one viewer's wistful thought.

Sixty-five posters from 40 countries are being displayed for an indefinite period on the first floor of the main building under the title "Travel: Then and Now."

THE SITUATION LEAD

Still another technique which is used to brighten an otherwise dull news story is the situation lead. The news writer emphasizes the effect of an event. The following example is from a UPI newspaper story:

OLYMPIA, Wash., (UPI) Voters won't know for a while whether they'll be voting to lower the drinking age in the state from 21 to 18 next November because somebody made off with the petitions bearing 107,000 signatures necessary to get the initiative on the ballot.

OTHER LEADS

There are many other types of news leads including those that begin with a question, quotation, or epigram. Many of these have been borrowed from magazine writers. A further discussion of leads follows in Chapter 11.

EXERCISES

1. Using the latest edition of a local or area newspaper, study the leads. List on separate paper the different techniques used by the writers to attract the reader's attention and to induce the reader to read the stories.

2. Listen to a local radio news program. If possible, tape-record the program. List on separate paper the different techniques used by the broadcast news writers to attract the listener's attention.

Chapter 9

The Body

Good journalistic writing is simply good writing.
There is no such thing as "journalese," a term
of scorn sometimes applied to the work of the
newspaperman.

Phillip H. Ault and Edwin Emery

The body of a news story further explains and expands upon the essential facts summarized by the lead. The body of the news story strengthens the lead.

In the body of the news story, the facts usually are presented in a descending order of importance. An example is the following story about Chicago Mayor Richard Daley's 70th birthday, written by Edward Schreiber for the **Chicago Tribune:**

Lead.. (1)

Four hundred top leaders in politics, business, and labor crowded into Mayor Daley's office yesterday for his biggest City Hall birthday party in his 17 years in office. He is 70 years old.

Body.. (2)

The mayor was presented with a huge cake, several inches tall and a yard square, with mostly chocolate frosting, except for a replica of the John Hancock Center in white. The cake was prepared by Pierre Orsi, executive chef of the 95th Restaurant in the center.

(3)

As Daley stood in front of the cake with his four sons, a group from the Fire Department Glee Club sang "Happy Birthday" and "When Irish Eyes Are Smiling."

(4)

"I suppose all of us get a little sentimental on our birthday," Daley then said. "We think of a lot of things. I was fortunate to have a good dad and mother. I've had a lot of fine people around me. I have a fine wife and family. I'm thankful for the friendships made."

(5) He expressed hope that in the decade of the 1970s "we can bridge the great gap which supposedly exists between the young and old."

(6) The mayor cut the first piece of cake, and it was moved near the entrance of his suite of offices. A number of city employees came in for cake as the dignitaries filed in to shake Daley's hand.

Paragraph (1) is the summary lead or intro. It contains the who, what, when, where, and why. Paragraphs (2) through (6) contain the body of the news story. Each paragraph is complete. An editor could, if necessary, cut the story after paragraph (2), (3), (4), or (5) without hurting the story's major elements.

The reader should carefully examine all story examples in this chapter and elsewhere in the book, paying particular attention to how the writers have connected the leads to the bodies of their stories. The connecting word or words or phrases that link the leads to the bodies are important to the unity of each story.

EXAMPLES

The following examples have been included to show how professional news writers construct and organize facts in the bodies of their stories:

Newspaper Stories

Lead

LOS ANGELES, Calif., (UPI) - A 21-year-old electronics expert who stole $1 million in equipment from the Pacific Telephone Company by tricking its computer for three years has been sentenced to two months in jail.

Body

Jerry N. Schneider was put on three years' probation on condition he refrain from buying or selling any telephone equipment.

With a phony telephone truck to haul the goods and an electronic device to order more, Schneider ran a thriving company that offered bargain-basement prices. A suspicious employee tipped off the district attorney's office and an investigation followed.

JEFFERSON CITY, Mo., (AP) - Former Missouri Gov. John M. Dalton died at a Jefferson City hospital today of cancer. He was 71 and had been ill for several months.

Mr. Dalton served eight years as attorney general before becoming governor in 1960. He was a Democrat from Kennett and earlier had been marshal of the Missouri Supreme Court.

Mr. Dalton's administration was marked by economy, but when the state ran shy of funds, he persuaded the legislature to increase the state sales tax from 2 to 3 cents on the dollar.

That gave his successor, Gov. Warren E. Hearnes, a running start on solving the state's problems.

A lawyer and cotton farmer in southeastern Missouri for years, Mr. Dalton had practiced law in Jefferson City since leaving office.

Survivors include his wife, the former Geraldine Hall; a son, John Hall Dalton, of Kennett; a daughter, Mrs. John W. Hyland, of Dallas, Tex., and five grandchildren.

The above story serves as an example of the typical news obituary.

SAN FRANCISCO, Calif., (UPI) - "I don't mind at all," said Jane Burnside as an agent for Pacific Southwest Airways rummaged through her bag of clothing. "I think there should be **some** check."

Carrying out President Nixon's order to commuter airlines for stricter anti-hijacking measures because of two hijackings of Pacific Southwest planes in two days, the agent pulled keys, makeup, and purse from the 23-year-old Menlo Park woman's handbag. Then, satisfied, he allowed her to board the plane for Sacramento.

Her reaction was typical of the passengers who stood in long lines Friday at San Francisco International Airport, scene of several hijackings, while their hand-carried luggage was searched.

Thomas Marks said he and his wife checked in two hours before departure time so United Air Lines would have plenty of time to screen them.

"I've had butterflies all day just thinking about this," said his wife as the couple waited in line to start a vacation trip to Yugoslavia.

But Marks said, "No one checked us as they should have done. We'll see just how good their checking methods are. I've got a travel iron in my bag and it should show up in the metal detector."

Passengers stepped one at a time through the parallel bars of the metal-detecting device, while a United employee kept an eye on the monitor. A security official stood outside a small booth where personal searches are made.

The Markses got through without their baggage being checked. The United employee smiled a greeting as they walked by him and onto the plane.

PSA officials were reluctant to talk about tightened security.

But passenger agents were asking the airline's customers to show their driver's licenses or other identification.

According to federal laws, airlines are supposed to use at least three or four check methods. They are: metal detection devices, spot checks of baggage, screening of passengers against the Federal Aviation Administration's profile of likely hijackers, and spot checks of passenger identification.

Young men, particularly with long hair, appeared to be singled out. Their pockets and bags were checked. A couple of youths were searched by a security official. An Army major in uniform had his small flight bag checked.

Lead

REDDING, Calif., (AP) - A flight plan marked "No Return" was found in the wreckage Tuesday of a small plane stolen by a man who performed loops and dives over his ex-girlfriend's home and then nosedived to his death, sheriff's deputies said.

Body

Victim Robert D. Lively, 25, formerly of Redding, apparently was despondent because his former girlfriend, who lived in Project City northeast of here, had married someone else, said Sgt. Don Acker.

Acker said Lively performed stunt tricks in the single-engine plane for almost four hours, although a deputy manning a ground-to-air radio warned him he was running out of gas.

Acker said Lively had filled out a flight plan marked: "Destination Project City. One way. No Return."

"He apparently was having problems with his old girlfriend who lived in Project City," Acker said. "So he created this scene either to scare her or whatever. He was advised he was running out of fuel, but he said he didn't care.

"He did in fact make a one-way flight," Acker added.

He said Lively stole the single-engine Avalon A-2 about 3 a.m. from nearby Enterprise Sky Park, where he had been taking pilot lessons.

Acker identified the girlfriend as Billy Joyce Kissinger. Her father refused to let reporters talk to her.

It sounds like he wanted to die, doesn't it?" said Lively's mother, Betty Lynch, who lives near Cupertino. Shasta County Sheriff's Dep. Jon Kelbaugh talked with Lively by radio for 15 minutes before the crash, urging him to land.

"I tried to talk him down but he wouldn't come down," said Kelbaugh, who had known Lively in Redding. He said Lively refused to explain his actions. Kelbaugh reported Lively's last words were:

"That's it. It's all over."

An eyewitness said the plane's engine suddenly stopped, the propeller started slowing down, and the plane nosedived near an abandoned private airstrip northeast of here. Lively was pronounced dead at the scene.

News stories can be very short. Sometimes the lead and body of a story may be contained in one paragraph. Such stories are called **shorts**.

Although shorts usually contain four or five sentences and one or two paragraphs, the following short has the lead and body in one sentence:

SAN FRANCISCO (AP) - A sign over the bar at a restaurant in North Beach announces, "We do not serve drunks of any race, creed, or color."

Such shorts are used to freshen the daily news routine.

BROADCAST STORIES

Broadcast news stories may not contain bodies. Most news stories used on short 5-minute radio news programs are only summaries—the essence of newspaper leads. Broadcast news stories, however, can and often do contain bodies, especially television news stories using visual material. An example is the story broadcast on the "CBS Evening News with Walter Cronkite" on April 5, 1971:

Cronkite: (on camera)	This was sick aunt and grandma's funeral day in Washington, opening day of the baseball season. Bob Schieffer had a good excuse for being there—we sent him.

This opening by Cronkite is the lead. It briefly summarizes the story and draws attention to the report from newsman Bob Schieffer, who followed with:

Schieffer: (voice over film) (visual material included silent newsfilm showing what Schieffer was describing.)	It was a standing-room-only crowd of 45,000 at RFK stadium; it included many Washington celebrities, among them Interior Secretary Rogers Morton, Agriculture Secretary Clifford Hardin. Senator Hubert Humphrey signed autographs. Usually, there are no speeches at the opening day ceremonies, but this year the White House dispatched Defense Secretary Laird to read a message from the President and to introduce Army Sergeant Daniel Pitzer. The crowd greeted Laird as if he were the umpire.
Sound Film: (ballpark announcer—indistinct) Sec. Laird: (on film)	For four long years, Sergeant Pitzer was a prisoner of the Viet Cong in South Vietnam. As he performs this American ritual of throwing out the first ball, he does so as a reminder that there are still a great many men in uniform, some 1600 of them, who have not seen a ball game in a long time, much less seen their homes or their families. Sergeant Pitzer also stands before you as a symbol of our deep and continuing national concern for the plight of these young men, and of our

| Schieffer: (voice over film) | national determination to hasten the day when they, too, can come home. Thank you. |
| | |

Schieffer: (voice over film)

The applause after Laird's speech was louder than the boos which preceded it. Sergeant Pitzer, who was released by the Viet Cong three years ago, got the biggest hand. He threw out the traditional first ball. It was a strike to Reggie Jackson of the Oakland team. Pitzer repeated the toss for photographers, going to the Senators' Paul Casanova with the second shot. The Senators lost the last 14 games of the season last year, but they jumped to an early lead today, putting two runs on the scoreboard in the bottom of the first inning. They went on to beat Oakland eight to nothing. It was the first time the Senators have won an opening game since 1962, today's win breaking an eight-game opening day losing streak.
Bob Schieffer, CBS NEWS, Washington.

In this story Bob Schieffer's portion was the body of the story. Schieffer, with the aid of visual material, told the story as it happened, in chronological order.

EXERCISES

1. Using the latest edition of a local or area newspaper, study the bodies of the longer news stories. Determine whether the writer has written complete paragraphs. Could the paragraphs be rearranged without hurting the clarity of the stories? Could the clarity of the stories be improved by rearranging the paragraphs in the bodies of the stories?

2. Listen to a local radio news program. If possible, tape-record the program. Study each news story. Are there bodies to the radio news stories? How are the leads written? Compare the construction of the radio news stories to the construction of the newspaper stories examined in exercise 1, above.

Chapter 10

Broadcast News Differences

It wasn't until radio really got
going that news reached Americans
in simple, direct English.
Paul W. White

The basic qualities of good news writing apply to print and broadcast news. Both forms stress compact sentences, and each selects and places words in a sentence for maximum effect. Paragraphs are usually short. Each paragraph is complete. All superfluous words, phrases, and clauses are eliminated. And there is conciseness, directness, and simplicity in good news writing, whether it is for print or broadcast. But there are differences. The print journalist, as has been pointed out, writes to be **read**. His copy must read well. The radio journalist writes to be **heard**. His copy must listen well. The television journalist also writes to be heard; but, because of the visual aspects of the medium, he often must consider both **sight** and **sound**.

TELEVISION NEWS WRITING

Television news writers probably write shorter news stories using fewer words than any other type of news writer. But do not get the impression that TV news writing is a snap. Mastering it is one of the most challenging jobs in the writing profession.

The key to good television news writing is to abstract the essence of a story and convey it in a minimum of time. The television news writer must boil everything down and be more direct. Literary style is out. Short, simple, declarative sentences are the key because the visual aspects of television news—still photographs, silent and sound motion picture film, video tape and other visuals—often tell much of the story. They create special problems for the television news writer, who must follow three basic rules:

(1) Do not cram your film or video tape narration full of details. If you do, the viewer is going to find it difficult to concentrate on what the narrator is saying and what is being shown in pictures. It is not necessary for the writer to explain what is clearly pointed out in the pictures. That is duplication. The written narration should tell the viewer only what he or she cannot learn from the pictures being shown.

(2) Relate your words to the pictures in telling the story. The narration and pictures must go hand in hand. The words heard and the pictures seen at any given time must correspond to each other.

(3) The news writer must carry the viewer into the story by telling it the way it happened. Although the narrator may begin with a summary lead before introducing visual material, the visual story that follows should be told in chronological order.

BASIC WRITING TECHNIQUES

When there is no visual material to help tell the story, the television news writer must produce the same kind of copy written by the radio journalist. It must convey the complete story in words and it must be written for the ear. Here are the basic writing techniques used to make radio and television news copy listenable:

Informality

Broadcast news copy, since it is read aloud, generally is more conversational than newspaper copy. Dean Miller, long-time UPI national radio news manager, once observed that the details of a broadcast story must be selected and placed on paper in such a way "as to create listener illusion that the announcer is 'back-fence talking' the facts in an authoritative yet entertaining way."

Compare the following news stories. The first was written for broadcast, the second a newspaper story:

This story was transmitted over the Associated Press
broadcast wire to radio and television clients shortly before
midnight on June 23, 1972.

Now compare the broadcast version to the following AP
newspaper story transmitted at about the same hour to
newspaper clients for use the following morning:

> A week of all but incessant rain was climaxed by a new storm
> yesterday as some of the worst floods on record ravaged the
> grievously stricken East from Virginia to upstate New York.
>   The National Weather Service saw no immediate end to the
> deluge, which it called a major disaster.
>   "I have never in my life seen such total destruction as has
> taken place in several areas of the state," Gov. Marvin Mandel of
> Maryland said after a helicopter survey. His state was one of five
> designated by President Richard Nixon as disaster areas.
>   Tropical storm Agnes moved up from the south early Wed-
> nesday, far enough inland to spare such cities as Philadelphia,
> Newark, and New York from major damage. Then a teeming
> successor drove in from the west. Combined, they claimed 79 lives,
> 31 of them in Pennsylvania alone. Scores were missing.
>   The damage was incalculable as raging river waters tore
> houses from their foundations, tossed motor cars about, and
> smashed pleasure craft. The most preliminary of estimates set
> damage at $160 million in Virginia alone, where commerce halted
> in flood areas, and stores, offices, and plants were abandoned.

This newspaper story was much longer than the broadcast
version above. There were 22 additional paragraphs containing much detail. In contrast, the AP broadcast version is
brief. It contains only the high points of the flood story. The
broadcast version is conversational. The newspaper version is
more formal. The print story is written in the inverted
pyramid form.

By reading both stories aloud, you will have a better understanding of the differences of writing news to be **read** and news to be **heard**. The lead sentence in the newspaper story is awkward when read aloud. It is much too long for a broadcast story. The broadcast lead contains 21 words compared to 33 words in the newspaper lead. That lead also lacks the feeling of immediacy which is conveyed by the broadcast version.

Tenses

Newspaper stories are often written in the past tense. Broadcast news copy should be written in the present or present perfect tense whenever possible. The active voice **tells** the story better and quicker. Compare the leads of the flood story:

Broadcast Lead

(NEW YORK) —— THE WORST FLOODS IN ITS HISTORY CONTINUE TO RAVAGE THE EASTERN SEABOARD, BRINGING THE TOLL IN WEATHER ATTRIBUTED DEATHS TO 79.

Newspaper Lead

A week of all but incessant rain was climaxed by a new storm yesterday as some of the worst floods on record ravaged the grievously stricken East, from Virginia to upstate New York.

In the broadcast lead the verbs **continue** and **bringing** (present tense) add freshness and the feeling of immediacy when the story is read aloud. But in the newspaper version the verb **climaxed** (past tense) and the word **yesterday** immediately date the story. It reads like old news.

Newspaper readers expect fresh news; however, they realize that newspapers do not have the immediacy capability of broadcasting. The past tense in the newspaper story is accepted. It is traditional. Readers understand that the newspaper story had to be written, the newspaper printed and then distributed. But it should be noted again, as was pointed out in the previous chapter, that many newspaper writers are beginning to write more timely leads, injecting some of the freshness that appears in good broadcast news copy.

Pronouns

Newspaper writers frequently use personal pronouns in news stories. They know their readers can reread the story with ease. But the broadcast journalist must be extremely careful with personal pronouns. Read the following story:

> A Smithville attorney has filed for governor. Fifty-four-year-old John W. Conner filed this morning at the state capital as an independent candidate for governor. **He** says he has entered the race because he feels it is time for a change in the governor's office.
> Commenting on the governor's race, **he** said the present governor, Democrat Bill Jones, has been in office far too long.
> **He** added that the Republican candidates offer very little hope for the state.

To the reader, this story is clear. You can refer back to see who **he** is. But read it aloud to a friend. The chances are that you will be asked **who** you are talking about. Candidate Conner's name appears only once in the story. If the listener misses the name the first time, there is no chance to learn **who** the story is about. Too many personal pronouns have been used. But by replacing those pronouns with Conner's name, the story's clarity improves:

> A Smithville attorney has filed for governor. Fifty-four-year-old John W. Conner filed this morning at the state capital as an independent candidate for governor. **Conner** says he has entered the race because he feels it is time for a change in the governor's office.
> Commenting on the governor's race, **Conner** said the present governor, Democrat Bill Jones, has been in office far too long.
> **Conner** added that the Republican candidates offer very little hope for the state.

Naming the Source

In many newspaper stories the identification or qualifying phrase is placed at the end of a sentence. Example:

> Washington (AP) —— A year's supply of "market basket" groceries cost consumers $5 more in May as a result of a $16 average increase for farmers and $11 price cutback among middlemen, the Agriculture Department said today.

The position of the qualifying phrase — "the Agriculture Department said today" — is acceptable in print. The eye can follow the story easily, read ahead if necessary to learn the source. But in broadcast news copy, such qualifying phrases should never dangle at the end of a sentence. It is awkward and not conversational.

Rewriting the newspaper lead for broadcast, the qualifying phrase appears at the beginning:

> The Agriculture Department says a year's supply of groceries cost consumers five dollars more in May.
> The department says an average increase of 16 dollars for farmers and an 11 dollar price cutback among middlemen was responsible for the increase.

By identifying the source of the story first, there is no doubt in the listener's mind as to the authority of the story.

The Associated Press tells its news writers that there is "a fine line between when to attribute and when not to attribute. Only experience and good judgment can supply the answer. But it is well to remember this: Always attribute anything which might be disputed by anybody at any time in the future."

Numbers

The eyes can play tricks on the broadcast journalist when he reads groups of numbers such as 6,245,483,244 or 22,639,428 on the air. The eyes have a difficult time translating such large groupings. To insure clarity and ease of reading, the broadcast journalist must write out difficult-to-read figures. The following rules are used by most broadcast news writers:

(1) Write out numbers one through nine.
(2) Use numerals for 10 through 999.
(3) For hundred, thousand, million, billion, write it:

16-hundred (not 1,600)
three-thousand (not 3,000)
16-thousand-250 (not 16,250)
eight-million (not 8,000,000)
four-billion-560 million (not 4,560,000,000)

Fig. 10-1. NBC News correspondent Edwin Newman. He began his career as a news writer. For a time he wrote for Eric Sevareid. Today, as an NBC News Correspondent, Newman writes much of the material he broadcasts. (Courtesy NBC.)

Newspaper writers do not hesitate to include figures in their news stories because the reader can easily absorb them or pass over those figures of little interest. But the broadcast news writer should use only those figures essential to the story. Too many numbers, statistics, and percentage figures can confuse listeners. To make certain this does not happen, the broadcast news writer should try to avoid including numbers, statistics, and percentages whenever possible. Only those figures essential to the meaning of the story should be used. And then, whenever possible, the broadcast news writer should round out figures. For example, the figures $162,258 should be written "more than 162-thousand dollars" unless the specific amount is essential to the meaning of the story.

The newspaper writer can write "a billion dollars." There is no question in the reader's mind as to the amount. But if the broadcast news writer writes "a billion dollars" in his copy, it may sound like "eight billion dollars" when read aloud on the air. In such cases the word **one** should be used in place of the letter a to guarantee absolute clarity.

The broadcast journalist should write dates in a conversational form such as June 1st, 10th, and 21st.

Ages

Newspapers follow the practice of including a person's age after the name. In broadcast copy a person's age **always** comes before the name. It helps to build a stronger word picture in the listener's mind. And it is more conversational. Example:

(a) Robert W. Johnson, 26, today told members of the state legislature...

(b) Twenty-six-year-old Robert W. Johnson today told members of the state legislature...

Example (a) is the newspaper form. It is not conversational. Example (b) is written for broadcast. It is easy on the ear.

Titles

Another standard practice in newspaper journalism is to place a person's title after his name. The opposite is the rule in broadcast news. The title should precede the name. It is not very conversational to say, "Richard M. Nixon, President of the United States." It sounds too formal. It is awkward. The broadcast news writer should simply write, "President Nixon."

Names

For clarity and accuracy, newspapers often use a person's full — first, middle, and last — in news stories. In broadcast news, middle names are usually deleted unless, as in the case of many prominent persons, the middle name has become closely identified with the person's name. For example, few persons would know the name William Hearst. But include the middle name of the late newspaper publisher and everyone would immediately recognize William Randolph Hearst.

The newspaper writer may start a lead sentence with the name of a person, but the broadcast news writer must never do so unless the name is that of a well known person. Most names should be delayed until the second sentence. Compare the following examples:

Wrong Way:

Twenty-six-year-old John W. Davis of Topeka has been killed in a two-car accident on the Kansas Turnpike near Kansas City.

The Kansas Highway Patrol says Davis died when he lost control of his auto and it struck another auto.

The occupants in the other car were not injured.

Right Way:

A Topeka man has been killed in a two-car accident on the Kansas Turnpike near Kansas City.

Dead is 26-year old John W. Davis.

The Kansas Highway Patrol says Davis died when he lost control of his auto and it struck another auto.

The occupants in the other car were not injured.

The name John W. Davis means little to the listener. Davis is not prominent. His name would not be instantly recognized by listeners. By using the name in the lead the writer will not catch the listener's attention when the story begins.

By delaying the name, the listener is attracted to the story. He will ask himself "What Topeka man has been killed?" and he will listen to learn who died. In the example above, the dead man's identity is told in the second sentence.

Meaningless Words

Newspaper writers can use **latter, former,** and **respectively** when referring to persons, places, or things already mentioned. But the broadcast news writer should never use them. The listener cannot refer back to a previous sentence or paragraph. These words are meaningless.

Another word that the broadcast news writer must be careful with is **here.** The word "here" to a person listening to a news program signifies only his own immediate location. If he is sitting in his home at Olpe, Kansas, and hears a newscaster tell of a tornado striking "here," he may head for the basement before realizing the news reporter is about 80 miles away in Topeka, Kansas.

Quotations

Quotes generally are used more sparingly in broadcast news copy than in newspaper copy because they tend to slow the pace of a newscast. In the early days of radio news the quotation mark was used out loud. Example:

> The Senator said—quote—"I have decided that I will not run again."—unquote.

Today the trend in broadcast journalism is to eliminate the words "quote" and "unquote" in news copy. Instead, broadcast news writers are alerting their listeners that an exact quotation is coming up by using such phrases as "in these words," "the senator added," "what he called" and so forth.

Many quotes are paraphrased. Paraphrases can be shorter and smoother. A really good quote, however, adds much authority to any broadcast news story. Should the broadcast news writer decide to paraphrase a quote, the speaker's exact meaning must be retained. The broadcast news writer should use neutral verbs in all direct quotations containing controversial material. The verbs says and declares usually come through objectively. Claims, points out, makes clear, insists, slaps down, and cracks have an editorial flavor.

EXERCISES

1. Watch your favorite network television news program. Pay particular attention to the narration of film or video-taped stories. Does the narration strengthen the stories? Does the narration duplicate what the viewer can see clearly in pictures? Rate each visual story with narration as good, fair, or poor.

2. Now watch your favorite local television news program. Follow the procedure outlined above. Rate each visual story with narration as good, fair, or poor.

Chapter 11

The Feature Story

I have no literary devices.
I know my facts thoroughly before I
begin to write, and then I try to tell
the story in the best way I can.
A. B. MacDonald

Every print and broadcast feature story usually has one thing in common: they each contain a strong element of human interest. The term "feature story" has been defined as a news story that may not affect the lives, welfare, or future of the readers or listeners, but which is interesting, entertaining, and informative.

There is a very thin line between the hard or spot news story and the feature story. Many news stories contain the ingredients of feature stories. Whether the final product is a feature or hard or spot news story depends upon the writer. It depends on how he plays the story.

Consider the story of two visitors from out of town who have their station wagon stolen while attending a convention in New Orleans. Normally, the story would merit a few sentences in the local newspaper or on the local radio news programs. As a news story it is routine. Many vehicles are stolen daily in every large city. But for the reporter who investigated the story and who looked beyond the police report, there was a feature story that was transmitted nationally by the Associated Press on their newspaper and broadcast wires. It read:

NEW ORLEANS, La., (AP) - The new station wagon of Mr. and Mrs. Albert Briles of Cedar Rapids, Iowa, was stolen after they arrived here for the convention of the National Association of Retail Grocers of the United States.

As the couple prepared to return home, they heard the results of the door prize drawing of the convention. The winners: Mr. and Mrs. Briles. The prize: a new station wagon.

LEAD

Attract interest to story

BODY

Sometimes written in chronological order but not always.

It should be written the best possible way to tell the story most effectively.

ENDING

Usually short

Fig. 11-1. The feature story form has a beginning, middle, and an end.

Newspaper feature stories are similar to hard or spot news stories. They require good writing and usually include a lead and a body, but unlike many news stories, the feature story generally has an ending. This is the main difference in the construction of the news feature story (Fig. 11-1).

Consider the organization of the following feature story written by the author for the Associated Press. It is reprinted here as it appeared in the **Chicago Daily News**, April 15, 1972:

Quotation lead KANSAS CITY, Mo. (AP) - Jesse Woodson James, outlaw, died on April 3, 1882.

Attracts On that day, as Billy Gashade's song tells,

reader's attention

Anniversary

James
today

Summary

Reader
is
taken
on
an
armchair
tour

"Robert Ford came along like a thief in the night. And laid poor Jesse in his grave."

That was 90 years ago.

Today the story of Jesse James is larger than life. The James legend exceeds James the man. Jesse James is perhaps the best known badman in all America.

More than 500 books and pamphlets have been written about him, plus a dozen motion pictures and a television series.

In Jesse James country—northwest Missouri—Jesse is alive in tradition and legend, thanks to private enterprise. There is the house where Jesse James was born, a restored bank museum where the James boys are said to have pulled the first daylight bank holdup in America, and the house where Jesse was killed. A few miles away is the grave where he is buried.

For the traveler who starts early, all of these sites can be seen in one day.

Along Highway 169 on the south side of St. Joseph, Mo., is the frame house where Jesse James was shot in the back by Bob Ford. Ray Miller owns the house, which has been in its present location 33 years. It was moved there in 1938 from a high bluff on the east side of town. Today it is next door to the Jesse James Motel.

"Several hundred persons visit the house each week," said Miller.

It is an unpainted dirty black frame structure perserved by linseed oil.

Just inside, visitors who pay the admittance fee see a framed piece of embroidery that reads "God Bless Our Home." Miller said Jesse was straightening such a frame, standing on a chair, when Bob Ford pulled his gun and shot him.

Below the frame is the bullet hole. Now under glass, it is probably 10 times its original size. Before the glass was installed many years ago, souvenir hunters cut, tore and chipped away pieces of plaster until today only a corner of what was the original bullet hole can be seen. It is marked by black crayon.

Leaving the house where Jesse James died, your next stop may be Kearney, Mo., along the Jesse James trail. It is about 45 miles away.

The first stop in Kearney is Mount Olivet Cemetery where Jesse James is buried in the family plot along with his wife, mother, stepfather, and half-brother.

Jesse James was buried here early in the century. Before that his body rested under a large coffee bean tree at the James farm home, the next stop.

The James farm home is about three miles northeast of Kearney. At the gate the visitor usually meets one of two grandsons of Jesse James. On Sundays both grandsons, Lawrence H. Barr, 69, and Forster R. Barr, 67, team up to conduct tours. The farm is still owned by the daughter-in-law of Frank James, Mae James, who now lives in a nursing home.

After paying an entrance fee, visitors to the house are told by the Barr brothers about Jesse James and the family's history, as they tour the kitchen, sitting room, and bedroom in the east wing.

Leaving the James farm home, the last stop along the Jesse James trail is Liberty, Mo., about a 20-minute drive south.

Following the signs it is easy to find the bank museum located on the northwest corner of the public square in the business district.

Inside the green-shuttered red brick building was the first daylight bank holdup in the United States. The date was Feb. 13, 1866, as noted on an outside wall plaque. It was placed there by the Liberty Chamber of Commerce in 1958. The robbery is attributed to the James gang.

Very Brief Ending
It was here in the Liberty bank building that Jesse James launched his career in crime, a career that ended 90 years ago on April 3, 1882.

FEATURE STORY LEADS

In Chapter 8 there is a discussion of the various techniques used to attract readers to the beginning of a news story. These techniques also apply to feature stories. Here are three examples used by the author in a series of feature stories written for the Associated Press:

Quotation lead

Attracts attention

COTTONWOOD FALLS, Kan., (AP)
"Mother nature's round, undulating breasts, soft and warm in the sunshine, restfully inviting and rich in the promise of nurture."

This description of the Kansas Flint Hills was written about 1945 by the late Kansas rancher, Dan Casement of Manhattan.

It is perhaps the best description of the Kansas Flint Hills—sometimes called the Bluestem Hills. Their beauty is hard to describe to anyone who has never viewed them in their glory.

The Flint Hills comprise about four million acres of eastern Kansas. They have none of the rich, flaming beauty of the forested New England mountains nor the austere majesty of the Rockies. The Flint Hills are prairie lands.

They stretch from north of Manhattan, Kan., southward into the Osage Hills of Oklahoma in a belt varying in width from 30 to 60 miles. They cover all or part of 19 counties in Kansas. Chase County and its county seat of Cottonwood Falls rest near the heart.

COFFEYVILLE, Kan., (AP) - On the morning of October 5, 1892, five armed horsemen rode into Coffeyville, Kan. They constituted the Dalton gang, and they were riding into their home town. Within 12 minutes they had robbed two banks of nearly $25,000 and were engaged in a shootout.

Today the Dalton raid is history. No one is alive who took part in it, or in the defense of the town. But the memories of that day are still alive in Coffeyville.

Two blocks north of the junction of highways 166 and 169 is a monument erected in 1949 to the memory of the four men who died fighting the outlaws. It stands on the plaza in the center of Coffeyville's business district.

Half a block to the east is the Dalton Museum. It, too, is dedicated to the four citizens who died.

The Dalton Museum exhibits include three saddles used by the outlaws, a single-action Colt 45 revolver carried by Bob Dalton, a sack used to carry the money from one of the banks, some of the outlaws' clothing, and even the threshold taken from the old First National Bank building over which two of the Daltons walked the morning of the robbery.

CHERRYVALE, Kan., (AP) - Two blocks east of highway 169 in Cherryvale, between Parsons and Independence in Southeastern Kansas, is the replica of a home of killers. It is the Bender Museum, a reproduction of the original Bender home and store that stood on the prairie eight miles northeast of Cherryvale 100 years ago.

The Cherryvale Chamber of Commerce opened the museum in May 1961, and several thousand tourists have visited the building annually, in summer months when it is open.

Inside the museum are 19th century furnishings, much like what the Benders must have had. Crude manikins, representing the Benders and a potential victim, give the impression that a murder is about to be committed.

On the south wall, encased in glass, is the wreath of human hair from Bender victims. It was woven by a Cherryvale woman after the victims were found in May 1873. In a showcase below are old newspaper clippings, books, photos, all concerned with the Bender's history.

Another type of feature story lead, used by the author in an article for **Star** Magazine, the Sunday supplement of **The Kansas City Star**, is the news summary lead. It is similar to the straight news story lead:

The annual spring spectacular is under way in the Kansas Flint Hills. From north of Manhattan south to the Oklahoma border and in a swath 30 to 50 miles wide, bluestem pastures are being burned. But not all pastures.

Each spring the controversy over burning has flared like the orange flames that sweep across many a bluestem pasture. But this spring the opposition in the hills is not as evident as in years gone by.

Today there is a better understanding of the advantages and disadvantages of burning.

Nearly all cattlemen raising steers firmly believe their pastures must be burned regularly if the grass is to be good and sufficient for their cattle. And nearly all of them are burning. But most cow-calf operators are not burning.

Why the different philosophy?

Do the cow-calf operators feel burning is harmful?

There are answers to these questions, but the answers are complex.

Still another type of lead for feature stories is the janus-faced lead which may look backward into the past or forward into the future for purposes of comparison. In the example below, the first three paragraphs of a story by the author that appeared in **The Kansas City Times**, the lead looks backward:

Contrast lead

It has been 91 years since open saloons were legal in Kansas, but names such as the Side Track, Buckhorn Tavern, Pearl, Saratoga, Star of the West, Alamo, Rowdy Joe's, Old Red's, and Longbranch have not passed from history.

More contrast

The modern-day version of a Kansas saloon, as pictured in Western movies or on television, sometimes lacks authenticity. Most old-time saloons in Kansas were not fabulous places of plush pleasure with block-long bars and regular floor shows featuring beautiful girls doing the can-can.

Detail

The very early saloons consisted of wood planks resting on two barrels in a tent or dugout or beside a wagon on the prairie near a military post. As Kansas grew after the Civil War, more permanent structures were built.

Another technique that can be used to attract readers is the dated lead. The author used such a lead in writing a historical feature for **The Kansas City Star** about Frederic Remington, the Western artist:

Word picture

It was late March, 1883.

The calendar said it was spring, and the rolling Kansas Flint Hills were showing their first green tint. But winter's chill was still in the air as the Santa Fe passenger train pulled into Peabody, Kan.

Details

For the stocky youth of 22 years who stepped off the train, the long journey from New York was over. Fred Remington had come to Kansas to "get rich" raising sheep. And rich he would become, but not in dollars.

123

Within two years, Remington's dream of material wealth would be shattered, and he would return East. But the young New Yorker would carry with him lasting impressions of life in Kansas and Kansas City; impressions that would greatly influence the work of Frederic Remington, artist of the Old West.

Feature writers are frequently asked, "Where do you get your ideas and material?" The answer is not simple. The feature article has been called the news writer's masterpiece because it often requires more research and writing and rewriting than the average news story. It takes a great deal of time to produce a good feature story.

There is no simple rule of thumb to follow to locating feature stories except, "keep your eyes and ears open." Feature material is everywhere. Ernest Hemingway once wrote, "Write about what you know and write truly. Write about people you know, that you love and hate, not about people you study about." If the feature writer will follow Hemingway's advice, he will, from the beginning, have more than a passing interest in the subject matter.

While many feature stories are the result of routine reporting or playing up a minor news event by accentuating the human-interest angle, many feature writers find their material in libraries. This is particularly true of the feature writer who enjoys writing seasonal stories or those dealing with an anniversary of a birth, death, or other event. The following list contains numerous feature story possibilities:

THE FEATURE WRITER'S CALENDAR

January

January 1: Birthday of Paul Revere (1735).Birthday of Betsy Ross (1752). Lincoln freed the slaves (1863).

January 4: Utah, 45th state, admitted into the Union (1896).

January 6: Birthday of Carl Sandburg (born in 1878, died 1967).

January 7: George Gershwin, 26, completed the piano score of his **Rhapsody in Blue** (1924).

January 10: Thomas Paine published his pamphlet, **Common Sense**, in Philadelphia (1776).

January 11: Birthday of Alexander Hamilton, American statesman (1757).

January 12: Birthday of Jack London, American writer (1876).

January 17: Birthday of Benjamin Franklin (1706).

January 18: United States Senate repealed the federal tax on oleo margarine (1950).

January 20: Inauguration Day, once every four years, for American presidents.

January 24: Discovery of gold in a branch of the Sacramento River near Coloma, California (1848).

January 29: Kansas, 34th state, admitted into the Union (1861).

January 30: "The Lone Ranger" radio program broadcast for the first time (1933).

February

February 1: Texas voted to secede from the Union (1861).

February 2: Ground Hog Day.

February 4: Congress approved the Interstate Commerce Act (1887).

February 7: Birthday of Charles Dickens, great English novelist and journalist (1812).

February 11: Thomas Alva Edison was born at Milan, Ohio (1847).

February 14: Oregon, 33rd state, admitted into the Union (1859).

February 15: Birthday of Susan B. Anthony, pioneer crusader for women's rights (1820).

February 18: Planet Pluto discovered by astronomer Clyde W. Tombaugh at Flagstaff, Arizona (1930).

February 20: President George Washington signed the first postal act (1792).

February 22: Birthday of George Washington (1732).

February 25: Birthday of Enrico Caruso, great operatic tenor (1873).

February 27: Birthday of John Steinbeck, American novelist (1902).

February 29: Leap Year, extra day that comes every four years.

March

March 1: Ohio, 17th state, admitted into the Union (1803).

March 2: Congress established Mount Rainier National Park, Washington (1899).

March 4: Original Inauguration Day in United States until 1937. Vermont, 14th state, entered the Union (1791).

March 5: Winston Churchill, in a speech at Westminster College, Fulton, Missouri, originated his famous phrase, "The Iron Curtain."

March 8: Birthday of Oliver Wendell Holmes, foremost American jurist of his time (1841).

March 10: First paper money in the United States was issued (1862).

March 14: Eli Whitney received a patent on his invention, the cotton gin (1794).

March 15: Maine, the 23rd state, admitted into the Union (1820).

March 21: Spring begins.

March 25: RCA began commercial production of color television receivers (1954).

March 27: Ponce de Leon discovered the east coast of Florida (1513).

March 30: Texas readmitted into the Union (1870).

April

April 1: April Fool's Day.

April 3: Jesse James was shot to death at St. Joseph, Missouri (1882).

April 5: Jess Willard, ex-cowboy from Kansas, knocked out Jack Johnson in the 26th round at Havana, Cuba, and won the world heavyweight boxing championship (1915).

April 7: Nebraska legislature enacted a statute providing for an 8-hour work day (1891).

April 9: Civil War ended when General Robert E. Lee surrendered to General Ulysses S. Grant at Appomattox (1865).

April 11: President Truman relieved General Douglas MacArthur of his command in the Far East. (1951).

April 12: President Roosevelt died at Warm Springs, Georgia (1945).

April 14: Pan-American Day.

April 15: President Abraham Lincoln died (1865).

April 17: Benjamin Franklin died in Philadelphia at 84 years of age (1790).

April 20: Adolf Hitler was born in Austria (1889).

April 26: Birthday of John James Audubon, naturalist, painter and writer (1785).

April 30: Louisiana, 18th state, admitted into the Union (1812).

May

May 1: William F. "Buffalo Bill" Cody staged his first "Wild West" show (1883).

May 5: Napoleon Bonaparte died (1821).

May 6: Birthday of Sigmund Freud (1856).

May 8: Official V-E (Victory in Europe) Day (1945).

May 10: Confederate Memorial Day, a legal holiday in North and South Carolina.

May 11: Minnesota, 32nd state, admitted into the Union (1858).

May 13: Birthday of Joe Louis, prize fighter (1914).

May 20: Birthday of Honoré Balzac, French novelist (1799).

May 25: Birthday of Ralph Waldo Emerson, poet, philosopher and essayist (1803).

May 29: Wisconsin, 30th state, admitted into the Union (1848).

May 31: Birthday of Walt Whitman, poet and author (1819).

June

June 1: Kentucky, 15th state, admitted into the Union (1792).

June 4: The Anti-Saloon League of America was organized in Ohio (1893).

June 6: Birthday of Nathan Hale, American patriot (1755).

June 8: Birthday of Frank Lloyd Wright, American architect (1869).

June 11: Charles A. Lindberg was welcomed home in Washington, D.C. after his historic flight across the Atlantic Ocean (1927).

June 14: Missouri Legislature adopted the "Missouri Waltz" as the official state song.

June 15: Arkansas, 25th state, admitted to the Union (1836).

June 17: Amelia Earhart became the first woman to fly across the Atlantic Ocean (1928).

June 19: The United States Government adopted the 8-hour day for all federal employees (1912).

June 21: Summer begins.

June 23: Congress created the Civil Aeronautics Authority to regulate air traffic (1938).

June 28: Congress made Labor Day a holiday for federal employees (1894).

June 30: Congress created the Department of Indian Affairs (1834).

July

July 1: Franklin Delano Roosevelt, governor of New York, nominated for the Presidency by the Democrats (1932).

July 2: Heavyweight boxing champion Jack Dempsey knocked out George Carpentier in Jersey City (1921).

July 3: Idaho, 43rd state, admitted into the Union (1890).

July 4: The Continental Congress, in Philadelphia, adopted the Declaration of Independence (1776).

July 6: First all-star baseball game was played in Chicago (1933).

July 8: General Douglas MacArthur was appointed United Nations commander in Korea (1950).

July 10: Howard Hughes, with a crew of four, completed his flight around the world in a total of 91 hours (1938).

July 11: General Dwight D. Eisenhower won the Republican nomination for President in Chicago (1952).

July 17: Florida was formally ceded by Spain to the United States (1821).

July 21: Birthday of Ernest Hemingway, writer, at Oak Park, Illinois (1899).

July 22: John Dillinger, "Public Enemy Number One," was shot and killed in Chicago (1934).

July 27: Orville Wright set a world record by staying aloft in an airplane over Fort Myer, Virginia, for one hour, 12 minutes, and 40 seconds (1909).

July 31: Senator Robert A. Taft of Ohio, majority leader of the United States Senate, died in New York City (1953).

August

August 1: The United States Atomic Energy Commission established (1946).

August 4: The beginning of the United States Coast Guard (1790).

August 5: Congress abolished flogging in the Army (1861).

August 8: President Harry Truman signed the ratification of the United Nations Charter (1945).

August 15: Will Rogers, humorist, and Wiley Post, aviator, killed near Point Barrow, Alaska (1935).

August 16: Babe Ruth, baseball star, died in New York (1948).

August 20: Alaska discovered by the Danish navigator, Vitus Jonas Bering (1741).

August 22: Birthday of Claude Debussy, French composer (1862).

August 25: President Harry S. Truman seized all railroads in the United States to forestall a general strike (1950).

August 28: The first radio "commercial" was broadcast over station WEAF in New York City (1922).

August 31: Birthday of Arthur Godfrey, radio and television star (1903).

September

September 2: Congress established the United States Department of the Treasury (1789).

September 6: One hundred and forty-nine Pilgrims departed Plymouth, England, aboard the Mayflower, heading for the New World (1620).

September 9: California, 31st state, admitted into the Union (1850).

September 11: Birthday of O. Henry (William Sydney Porter), writer (1862).

September 14: The words of "The Star-Spangled Banner" were written by Francis Scott Key (1814).

September 16: Cherokee Strip Day in Oklahoma (1893).

September 18: President George Washington laid the cornerstone of the United States Capitol Building in Washington, D.C. (1793).

September 21: Birthday of H.G. Wells, English historian and novelist (1866).

September 23: Autumn begins.

September 25: Birthday of William Faulkner, American writer (1897).

September 30: President Dwight D. Eisenhower named California Governor Earl Warren chief justice of the United States Supreme Court (1953).

October

October 1: General Francisco Franco became head of Spain's nationalist government (1936).

October 6: Mormons renounced the practice of polygamy in Utah (1890).

October 7: Birthday of James Whitcomb Riley, poet (1849).

October 9: Chicago fire (1871).

October 12: Columbus Day (1492).

October 14: Brithday of Dwight D. Eisenhower (1890).

October 16: Birthday of Eugene O'Neill, American playwright (1888).

October 22: General Sam Houston became the first president of the Republic of Texas (1836).

October 26: Former heavyweight champion Joe Louis was knocked out by Rocky Marciano in New York City (1951).

October 30: National panic was caused when Orson Welles broadcast "The War of the Worlds" over CBS Radio (1938).

October 31: Nevada, 36th state, admitted into the Union (1864).

November

November 1: Two Puerto Rican Nationalists tried to assassinate President Harry S. Truman at the Blair House in Washington, D.C. (1950).

November 3: Frank D. Roosevelt defeated Alfred M. Landon in the presidential election (1936).

November 7: Jeannette Rankin, of Montana, won election and became the first congresswoman in history (1916).

November 8: Allied soldiers invaded North Africa (1942).

November 11: Washington, the 42nd state, admitted to the Union (1889).

November 15: Explorer Zebulon Pike sighted the mountain peak that is known as "Pike's Peak" (1806).

November 19: President Abraham Lincoln delivered his Gettysburg Address (1863).

November 26: President George Washington set aside this date as a day of national thanksgiving for the adoption of the United States Constitution (1789).

November 29: First Army-Navy football game held at West Point (1890).

December

December 1: Father Edward Flanagan founded Boys Town west of Omaha, Nebraska (1917).

December 2: John Brown hanged at Charlestown, Virginia (1859).

December 3: Illinois, 21st state, admitted to the Union (1818).

December 5: Birthday of Walt Disney, cartoonist (1901).

December 7: Japanese attacked Pearl Harbor, Hawaii (1941).

December 8: United States declared war, the beginning of World War II for this country (1941).

December 10: Mississippi, 20th state, admitted into the Union (1817).

December 14: Alabama, 22nd state, admitted into the Union (1819).

December 16: Birthday of Ludwig van Beethoven, German composer (1770). Boston Tea Party (1773).

December 19: Benjamin Franklin began to publish his **Poor Richard's Almanac** (1732).

December 22: Winter begins.

December 23: George Washington resigned from the army and retired to Mount Vernon (1783).

December 24: Birthday of Christopher "Kit" Carson, American frontiersman (1809).

December 25: Christmas.

December 27: Carrie Nation, anti-saloon leader, smashed a saloon in Wichita, Kansas (1900).

December 28: Birthday of Woodrow Wilson (1856).

December 30: Birthday of Rudyard Kipling, British poet and writer (1865).

December 31: New Year's Eve.

This partial list of historic events will provide the aspiring feature writer with many ideas for stories, but such material requires much work and thought. If the writer begins many weeks in advance of the anniversary, there will be sufficient time to thoroughly research the subject, obtain photographs and to write the polished story. Editors require such features well in advance of anniversary dates.

Although this chapter has centered around newspaper feature stories, the same elements apply to a broadcast news feature. In television, however, consideration must be given to the use of visual material which, as was pointed out in Chapter 10, often eliminates the need for written copy that duplicates what the viewer can understand from film or slides. The CBS News script, reprinted in Chapter 9, is a good example of a television feature story pegged to a news event.

E X E R C I S E

1. Obtain a large scrapbook. Start a collection of newspaper feature stories. Read the local and area newspapers with care. Select and clip those feature stories that appeal to you. Paste them in your scrapbook. Study how the stories are constructed. Try to isolate the various techniques used by the writers to attract and hold readers.

Chapter 12

Editing the Story

To stumble twice against the same
stone is a proverbial disgrace.

Cicero

Editing is defined as the process of making written material suitable for publication or presentation. In newspapers and broadcast news operations, the initial editing process is similar. It begins with the news writer. He carefully checks his story after it is written. If he discovers a misspelled word, a wordy sentence that needs to be compressed, a factual error or other mistake, they are corrected. From this point the editing process differs in print and broadcast news.

NEWSPAPER EDITING

When the newspaper writer is satisfied with his own editing of the story, he passes it along to the copy desk. There the copyreader reads the story. The copyreader, usually an experienced editor, may make additional changes. He may do one or more of the following things:

(1) Insure the accuracy of the story and inprove the news writer's copy when possible.

(2) Eliminate any libelous statements.

(3) Correct any mistakes in grammar, spelling, and punctuation.

(4) Make certain that the copy is fair and in good taste.

(5) Simplify and condense wordy copy to make it clear, compact, and interesting.

(6) Make all copy conform to the newspaper's style.

(7) Reject or revise old or biased news, advertising matter disguised as news, and trivial, trite, and dull words and phrases.

(8) Delete all editorializing and elements of bad taste in news stories.

After the story passes the inspection of the copyreader, it is sent to the print shop to be set in type. Later, a proof of the story—a reproduction on paper of the story in type—is sent to a proofreader. There the proof story is read.

At this point, proofreading is strictly mechanical. Its purpose is to see that the typesetter has set the copy as it was sent to him. The proofreader does not edit or change the copy. As a rule, improvements in copy, afterthoughts, or corrections in the original copy are not made at this time.

The proofreader makes all corrections clear and easy to see. The proof corrections are always written in the margin of the galley proof, not in the type proof itself.

Editing and Proofreading Symbols

Down through the years, editors have developed an elaborate set of symbols—shorthand signs—to facilitate the correcting of copy and instructing printers. One set of symbols (Fig. 12-1) is used by the news writer and the copy reader to correct the typewritten story, while the other set (Fig. 12-2) is used to correct the printer's proofs. The two should not be confused or used interchangeably.

BROADCAST NEWS EDITING

The process of editing news copy for radio and television often ends with the writer. Except in large broadcast news operations, the writer usually is the person who broadcasts what he writes. Editors and copyreaders are uncommon in small and medium sized broadcast newsrooms.

Because the broadcast news writer may be the only editor of his news copy, he must be extremely careful. Each story must be carefully copyread and corrected for accuracy, punctuation, spelling, grammar, style, taste, and libel. The copy must be clean. If many editing changes are required in the typed copy, the story should be retyped. Too many editing changes may distract the on-air newsman and cause reading difficulties. Most copyreading symbols used by newspaper editors cannot be used by broadcast newsmen. They tend to clutter the broadcast copy. Broadcast journalists, therefore, tend to use a more simplified system for editing. There are three basic functions of broadcast news editing:

¶	ATLANTA—When organization of	paragraph
⟋or	is over. ⎡Now it will be the first	paragraph
	the last attempts.⎦	
	⎡With this the conquering is to	no paragraph
or ⟋	according to ~~the~~ this compendi-	elisions
	the ⎡Jones⎦⎡Smith⎦ firm is not in the	transpose
	over a period of ⟨sixty⟩ or more in	use figures
	there were ⟨9⟩ in the party at the	spell
	Ada⟨Oklahoma,⟩ is in the lead at	abbreviate
	the ⟨Ga.⟩ man is to be among the	spell
	prince edward said it is his to	capitals
	accordingly ⧸This will be done	lower case
	the acc‿user pointed to them	join
	in⎸these times it is necessary to	separate
	the order for the ~~later~~ *Stet* devices	retain
BF/c or BF ⎤	⎤ By DONALD AMES ⎣	bold (black) face centered
	J. R. Thomas⎦	flush right
	⎣A. B. Jones Co.	flush left
	president ⋀is in a fine situation	caret
⌗	space (also 30 at end of item)	
⟋⟍ ⟋⟍⟍	quotation marks, apostrophe	
⟋	comma	
⊗ or ⊙	period	
⸗	hyphen	
⊢⊣	dash	
	a u n t (underline a u)	
	d o n e (overline o n)	

Fig. 12-1. Generally accepted copy marking symbols.

(1) **Misspelled words**: If a word is misspelled, the writer should cross out the entire word and spell it correctly (always print) in the space above. The same is true of words with transposed letters or characters. This makes for easier reading on the air. The broadcast newsman does not have time to interpret complicated editing marks while broadcasting the news. (See Fig. 12-3.)

(2) **Punctuation**: In adding a comma to a sentence, do not use the caret with the comma in the open end as used by newspaper copyreaders. Simply add the comma without any other mark. The same rule applies to quotation marks, periods, apostrophes, and other punctuation.

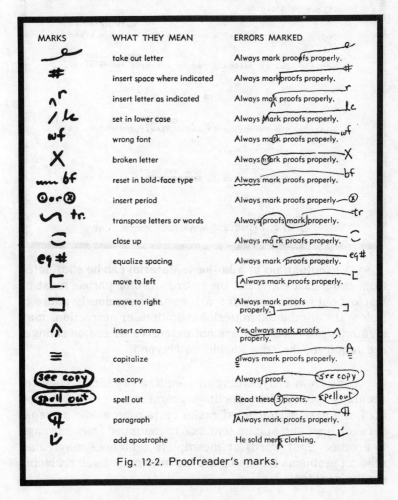

MARKS	WHAT THEY MEAN	ERRORS MARKED
	take out letter	Always mark proofs properly.
#	insert space where indicated	Always mark proofs properly.
^ r	insert letter as indicated	Always mak proofs properly.
/ lc	set in lower case	Always Mark proofs properly.
wf	wrong font	Always mark proofs properly.
X	broken letter	Always mark proofs properly.
~~ bf	reset in bold-face type	Always mark proofs properly.
⊙ or ⊗	insert period	Always mark proofs properly.
⌒ tr.	transpose letters or words	Always proofs mark properly.
⌒	close up	Always ma rk proofs properly.
eq #	equalize spacing	Always mark proofs properly.
⊏	move to left	Always mark proofs properly.
⊐	move to right	Always mark proofs properly.
^	insert comma	Yes always mark proofs properly.
≡	capitalize	always mark proofs properly.
see copy	see copy	Always proof.
spell out	spell out	Read these 3 proofs.
¶	paragraph	Always mark proofs properly.
'	add apostrophe	He sold mens clothing.

Fig. 12-2. Proofreader's marks.

```
   Misspelled Words:

      Bad:    President Nixͦn said he will not...

      Good:   President ̶N̶i̶x̶o̶n̶ said he will not...

   Punctuation:

      Bad:    Secretary of State Rogers, however‸will not go...

      Good:   Secretary of State Rogers, however, will not go...

   Eliminations or Additions:
                                          parking lot
      Bad:    Police seized a man in a nearby st‸re after...

                                          (parking lot)
      Good:   Police seized a man in a nearby ▬▬▬ after...

                              or

                            maker
      Bad:    The Pennsylvania law-br‸ker predicts an easy

              victory for...

                            law-maker
      Good:   The Pennsylvania ▬▬▬▬▬▬▬ predicts an easy

              victory for...
```

Fig. 12-3. Broadcast news copy corrections.

(3) **Eliminations or additions**: Material can be eliminated from broadcast copy, but the entire word or phrase must be blacked out so the newsman will not subconsciously pause to look at the eliminated material. Additions or corrections may be made, provided they are not extensive. If major changes are required, the copy should be retyped.

Aside from copyreading and editing broadcast copy for accuracy, punctuation, spelling, grammar, style, taste, and libel, the news writer must make certain no words are split between lines and that no sentence is continued from one page to another. Split words or incomplete sentences may cause reading problems for the on-the-air newsman. Such problems can be avoided.

Chapter 13

Law and the News Writer

Laws too gentle are seldom obeyed;
too severe, seldom executed.
Benjamin Franklin

The first amendment of the Constitution guarantees freedom of the press in a wide, general way. The amendment reads:

Congress shall make no law respecting an establishment of religion, or prohibiting the free exercise thereof; or abridging the freedom of speech, or of the press; or the right of the people peaceably to assemble, and to petition the Government for a redress of grievances.

Simply defined, the first amendment means there will be no censorship prior to publication. Today, this amendment is interpreted to include broadcasting. However, it does not permit unlimited dissemination of information. There are certain rights, privileges, and considerations that protect the public. The news writer must be aware of these.

PRIVACY AND LIBEL

While newspapers, news magazines, radio and television stations, and CATV operations have the right to report public business in the public interest, every citizen has the right to live his private life as he wants to. In legal terms this is the "right to privacy."

There have been relatively few suits brought against broadcast stations charging invasion of privacy. The majority of such cases have historically involved newspapers and magazines. But in recent years there has been some concern about television and the right to privacy. Television film cameras go many places. Many television news directors warn their photographers to be cautious and not to violate a citizen's right to privacy.

Journalism's biggest legal threat is libel. If a newspaper or broadcast station reports an untrue story which exposes a person or group of persons to public hatred, contempt, or ridicule, and if the story unjustly defames the character of an individual or hurts his business, the story is considered libelous. Such a story can lead to a civil court suit for which damages may be recovered. Libel also may be a crime, but indictments for criminal libel with a possible fine and imprisonment are not very common.

Often there is confusion between libel and slander. Libel is written or printed; slander is oral. Defamation resulting from a radio or television news story is usually considered libel since most broadcast news is written.

Most cases of libel are caused by negligence and most occur in the handling of court news, especially from criminal courts. The news writer must be extremely careful in reporting the names of suspects in crime stories and make certain that an individual has been arrested or charged before using the names in print or on the air. However, it is possible to libel a person if, even though you do not use his name, your description readily identifies him.

The news writer's rules for avoiding libel are simple. Ask the following questions when writing a news story:

(1) Am I being fair to the person or persons involved?
(2) Is this the truth and can I prove it?
(3) Is the story privileged information?

Certain words and expressions can lead to libel suits. While the news writer can use the descriptive words listed below, he must use them with care, making certain they are appropriate:

abductor	bribery	deserter
abortionist	burglar	drunkard
adulterer	common drunk	embezzler
anarchist	conspirator	extortionist
arson	criminal	false pretenses
bigamist	dead beat	forger
blackmailer	degenerate	fornication

fraud	insane	prostitute
gambler	kidnaper	quack
grafter	liar	rape
homicide	mistress	robber
hypocrite	murderer	shyster
incest	nigger	sodomist
indecent exposure	perjury	swindler
informer	whore	

PRIVILEGED INFORMATION

Privileged information is that which the public is entitled to know. It includes all official proceedings of city council meetings, state legislatures, the actions taken by Congress and other such legislative bodies. Privileged information gives the news writer certain immunities or freedom from liability if a person or a group of persons is libeled in such meetings.

For example, a member of Congress is not liable for statements made by him in the discharge of his official duties. Likewise, libelous statements made in the course of legal proceedings, by participants therein, are privileged, but privilege is conditional and not absolute. Stories written from such public sources must be complete, accurate, fair, and impartial. They must be free of comments and must not contain malice.

CONTEMPT

News writers have no immunity from contempt charges. The courts have the power to cite and punish anyone for contempt. A news writer could be held in contempt if a judge decides the writer has interfered with the administration of justice. The offense may range from talking in the courtroom, to taking motion pictures, to writing a news story which might jeopardize a defendant's right to a fair trial. Contempt usually is defined as either direct or indirect.

Direct contempt is committed in the presence of the court. There are four reasons why a reporter may be cited for direct contempt:

(1) Disobeying a court order.

(2) Refusing under oath to disclose a news source unless a state law grants him immunity from disclosing sources.

(3) Attempting to influence the testimony of any witness or the judge's decision.

(4) Disturbing the court process in any way.

Indirect contempt is committed outside the courtroom. In the case of the news writer, it usually concerns a published or broadcast news story. There are three reasons why a reporter may be cited for indirect contempt:

(1) A published or broadcast news story dealing with a trial which the court considers prejudicial because it is grossly false or inaccurate.

(2) Any news story which might discredit the court, thereby causing it to lose face in the public eye.

(3) A news story which might affect the decision in a pending case.

Many journalists feel that the contempt process is a restriction on the freedom of the press. Until recently most reporters felt they should have the right to withhold identity of news sources in the same sense that a medical doctor is immune from divulging details of patient relationship. But in June, 1972, the U.S. Supreme Court held, in a 5-to-4 decision, that constitutional guarantees of freedom of speech and freedom of the press are not abridged when newsmen are required to testify before grand juries, state or federal.

While the number of indirect contempt citations is relatively small, there is always the possibility that a newsman can be cited. In such cases, the reporter should remember that in an earlier ruling the U.S. Supreme Court has said there must be a "clear and present danger" that a news story or editorial will, in fact, interfere with the orderly process of justice. This means that a judge must have substantial evidence of this danger before he can use his contempt power.

CANON 35

News photographers, print and broadcast, are familiar with Canon 35. While it is not a law (it is one of the American

Bar Association's Canons of Judicial Ethics), it has had the effect of a law in many courts of the land. Canon 35 reads:

Proceedings in court should be conducted with fitting dignity and decorum. The taking of photographs in the courtroom during sessions of court or recesses between sessions, and the broadcasting or televising of court proceedings detract from the essential dignity of the proceedings, distract participants and witnesses in giving testimony, and create misconceptions with respect thereto in the mind of the public and should not be permitted.

In simple terms, Canon 35 bans still and motion picture photographs and video and audio recording of nearly all court proceedings. Some judges interpret Canon 35 as including empty courtrooms and the halls and corridors near the courtrooms. But not all judges adhere strongly to Canon 35. It depends upon the judge.

Appendix I

AP-UPI Newspaper Style

In 1960, at the suggestion of many newspapers, The Associated Press and United Press International collaborated on a common newspaper style for the two news services. The guidelines that follow have since become standard in many newspapers. The author wishes to thank The Associated Press for permission to reprint the following material.

Capitalization I

1.1 CAPITALIZE titles preceding a name: Secretary of State John Foster Dulles. LOWER CASE title standing alone or following a name: John Foster Dulles, secretary of state. EXCEPTION: Incumbent president of the United States is always capitalized. Do not capitalize candidate for president, no president may seize, etc.

1.2 CAPITALIZE government officials when used with name as title: Queen Elizabeth II, Premier Debre, etc. LOWER CASE when standing alone or following a name: Debre, premier of France.

1.3 CAPITALIZE Pope in all usage; pontiff is lower case.

1.4 CAPITALIZE foreign religious leader titles Imam, Patriarch, etc., but LOWER CASE standing alone or following a name. EXCEPTION: Pope and Dalai Lama, capitalized in all usage. (See Section VIII)

1.5 CAPITALIZE titles of authority before name but LOWER CASE standing alone or following a name: Ambassador John Jones; Jones, ambassador; the ambassador. (See 1.12, 3.31)

1.6 Long titles should follow a name: John Jones, executive director of the commercial department of Blank & Co. Richard Roe, secretary-treasurer, Blank & Co. (See 6.5)

1.7 LOWER CASE occupational or "false" titles such as day laborer John Jones, rookie left-handed pitcher Bill Wills, defense attorney John Jones. (See 2.14)

1.8 CAPITALIZE Union, Republic, Colonies referring to the United States; Republic of Korea, French Fifth Republic. (See 2.12)

1.9 CAPITALIZE U.S. Congress, Senate, House, Cabinet; Legislature when preceded by name of state; City Council; Security Council. LOWER CASE when standing alone: The legislature passed 300 bills.
The building is the Capitol, the city is capital.
Do not capitalize "congress" when it is used as a synonym for convention. (See 1.20)

1.10 CAPITALIZE committee in full names: Senate Judiciary Committee, House Ways and Means Committee, etc. LOWER CASE "subcommittee" in titles and standing alone, also "committee" standing alone.
In some shortened versions of long committee names, do not capitalize: Special Senate Select Committee to Investigate Improper Labor-Management Practices often is rackets committee, not capitalized.

1.11 CAPITALIZE full titles: Interstate Commerce Commission, New York State Thruway Authority, International Atomic Energy Authority, etc., LOWER CASE authority, commission, etc., standing alone. (See 2.1)

1.12 CAPITALIZE Supreme Court, Juvenile Court, 6th U.S. Circuit Court of Appeals, etc. (See 4.2) Specify which U.S. Court such as district, patent, tax, etc. It is Juvenile Court Judge John Jones and not Juvenile Judge John Jones.

1.13 CAPITALIZE Social Security (Administration, Act) when referring to U.S. system: He was receiving Social Security payments. LOWER CASE use in general sense: He was an advocate of social security for old age.

1.14 CAPITALIZE U.S. armed forces: Army (USA), Air Force (USAF), Navy (USN), Marines (USMC), Coast Guard, National Guard but LOWER CASE all foreign except Royal Air Force (RAF) and Royal Canadian Air Force (RCAF); French Foreign Legion, no abbreviation.
CAPITALIZE Marine, Coast Guardman, Swiss Guard, Evzone, Bengal Lancer, etc. LOWER CASE soldier, sailor, etc. NOTE: It is Coast Guardman (no "s") if member of U.S. Coast Guard.
CAPITALIZE Irish Republican Army (political). (See 1.20)

1.15 CAPITALIZE Joint Chiefs of Staff but LOWER CASE chiefs of staff.

1.16 CAPITALIZE holidays, historic events, ecclesiastical feasts, fast days, special events, hurricanes, typhoons, etc. Mothers Day, Labor Day, Battle of the Bulge, Good Friday, Passover, Christmas, Halloween, National Safety Week, Hurricane Hazel, Typhoon Tilda, New Year's (Day, Eve) but LOWER CASE: What will the new year bring? At the start of the new year, etc.

1.17 CAPITALIZE Antarctica, Arctic Circle but not antarctic or arctic.

1.18 CAPITALIZE specific regions: Middle East, Mideast, Middle West, Midwest, Upper Peninsula (Michigan), Southern (Illinois, California) Texas (Oklahoma) Panhandle, Orient, Chicago's near South Side, Loop, etc.

1.19 CAPITALIZE ideological or political areas: East-West, East Germany, West Germany. LOWER CASE mere direction: Snow fell in western North Dakota.

1.20 CAPITALIZE political parties and members but not "party." Democrat, Democratic, Republican, Socialist, Independent, Nationalist, Communist, Congress (India) etc. LOWER CASE democratic form of government, republican system, socialism, communism, etc.

CAPITALIZE Red when used as political, geographic, military, etc., descriptive.

LOWER CASE nationalist in referring to a partisan of a country.

CAPITALIZE Algerian Liberation Front (FLN) and Irish Republican Army (IRA). (See 1.14)

1.21 CAPITALIZE names of fraternal organizations: B'nai B'rith (no abbreviation), Ancient Free & Accepted Masons (AF&AM), Knights of Columbus (K. of C. as departure from 2.1). (See 2.5)

1.22 CAPITALIZE Deity and He, His, Him denoting Deity but not who, whose, whom. CAPITALIZE Talmud, Koran, Bible and all names of the Bible, confessions of faith and their adherents. (See Section VIII)

CAPITALIZE Satan and Hades but not devil and hell.

1.23 CAPITALIZE Civil War, War Between the States, Korean War, Revolution (U.S. and Bolshevik), World War I, World War II, etc.

1.24 CAPITALIZE names of races: Caucasian, Chinese, Negro, Indian, etc. LOWER CASE black, white, red (See 1.20), yellow. Do NOT use "colored" for Negro except in National Association for the Advancement of Colored People. Colored is correct in African usage.

Identification by race should be made when it is pertinent.

1.25 CAPITALIZE common noun as part of formal name: Hoover Dam, Missouri River, Barr County Courthouse. LOWER CASE dam, river, courthouse, etc., standing alone. CAPITALIZE Empire State Building, Blue Room, Carlton House (hotel), Carlton house (home), Wall Street, Hollywood Boulevard. (See 4.1)

Plurals would be: Broad and Main streets.

1.26 CAPITALIZE species of livestock, animals, fowl, etc., but LOWER CASE noun: Airedale, terrier, Percheron, horse; Hereford, whiteface, etc.

1.27 CAPITALIZE names of flowers: Peace rose, etc. If Latin generic names are used CAPITALIZE the genus (camellia, Thea japonica).

1.28 CAPITALIZE trade names and trademark names: Super Sabre Jet, Thunderjet, but Boeing 707 jet (jet descriptive, not part of name), Pan Am Clipper.

"Coke" is a registered trademark of Coca-Cola and is not a synonym for soft drinks. "Thermos" is a registered trademark. Use vacuum bottle (flask, jug) instead.

Use generic, or broad, term preferably in all trademark names.

1.29 Some proper names have acquired independent common meaning and are not capitalized. They include paris green, dutch door, brussels sprouts, etc. Check dictionary.

1.30 CAPITALIZE titles of books, plays, hymns, poems, songs, etc., and place in quotation marks: "The Courtship of Miles Standish." (See 3.26)

The words a, in, of, etc., are capitalized only at the start or end of a title: "Of Thee I Sing" and "All Returns Are In" as examples.

1.31 CAPITALIZE first word of a quotation making a complete sentence after a comma or colon: Franklin said, "A penny saved is a penny earned." (See 3.16)

1.32 CAPITALIZE names of organizations, expositions, etc., Boy Scouts, Red Cross, World's Fair, Iowa State Fair but LOWER CASE scout, fair standing alone.

1.33 CAPITALIZATION of names should follow the use of preference of the person. In general, foreign particles are lower case when used with a forename, initials or title: Charles de Gaulle, Gen. de Gaulle, but De Gaulle without forename or title. (See 3.5, 6.4)

In anglicized versions the article usually is capitalized: Fiorello La Guardia.

It is E. I. du Pont de Nemours and Du Pont; Irenee du Pont but Samuel F. Du Pont (his usage).

1.34 CAPITALIZE fanciful appellations: Buckeye State, Leatherneck, Project Mercury, Operation Deep Freeze (Deepfreeze, one word, is trademark.)

1.35 CAPITALIZE decorations, awards, etc. Medal of Honor, Nobel Peace Prize.

Abbreviations II

2.1 First mention of organizations, firms, agencies, groups, etc., should be spelled out. Exception: AFL-CIO. In names that do not have commonly known abbreviations, the abbreviation should be bracketed after the spelled name. Thereafter in the story the abbreviation may be used. Example:

The desire was expressed in the Inter-American Economic and Social Council (IA-ECOSOC) of the Organization of American States (OAS) in considering the European Economic Cooperation Organization (ECCO).

Distant Early Warning line (DEW line).

General Agreement of Tariffs and Trade (GATT).

2.2 ABBREVIATE time zones, airplane designations, ships, distress call, military terms, etc. EDT, CST, MIGI7, B60, Military Police (MP), absent without official leave (AWOL), SOS (but May Day), USS Iowa, SS Brasil. (See 3.3, 10.12, 6.15)

2.3 ABBREVIATE business firms: Warner Bros.; Brown Implement Co.; Amalgamated Leather, Ltd.; Smith & Co., Inc. (See 3.40)

2.4 ABBREVIATE St., Ave., Blvd., Ter., in addresses but not Point, Port, Circle, Plaza, Place, Drive, Oval, Road, Lane. Examples:

16 E. 72nd St. (single "E" with period); 16 Gregory Ave. NW (no periods in "NW"); Sunset Boulevard, Main Street, Fifth Avenue (no addresses. (See 1.25, 4.1)

2.5 Lower case abbreviations usually take periods. The rule of thumb is if the letters without periods spell words, periods are needed. Examples: c.o.d., f.o.b., etc. However, m.p.h., a.m., p.m.

Periods are not needed in 35mm (film), 105mm (armament), ips (tape recording).

In news stories first mention of speed should be "miles an hour" or "miles per hour" and thereafter in story use m.p.h.

ABBREVIATE versus as vs. (with period).

2.6 ABBREVIATE states which follow cities (towns, villages, etc.), airbases, Indian agencies, national parks, etc. (See 3.23)

2.7 Standard abbreviations for states (rule of thumb is abbreviate none of six letters or less except Texas):

Ala.	Ill.	Miss.	N.M.	Tenn.
Ariz.	Ind.	Mo.	N.Y.	Tex.
Ark.	Kan.	Mont.	Okla.	Vt.
Calif.	Ky.	Neb.	Ore.	Va.
Colo.	La.	Nev.	Pa.	Wash.
Conn.	Md.	N.C.	R.I.	Wis.
Del.	Mass.	N.D.	S.C.	W.Va.
Fla.	Mich.	N.H.	S.D.	Wyo.
Ga.	Minn.	N.J.		

Do not abbreviate Alaska, Hawaii, Idaho, Iowa, Ohio, Maine or Utah.

All states are spelled standing alone: He went to Minnesota at the turn of the century.

2.8 ABBREVIATIONS:

C.Z.	P.R.	V.I.	Alta.	B.C.	Man.	N.S.
Que.	Ont.	Sask.	Nfld.	N.B.	B.W.I.	P.E.I.

but obscure ones should be spelled in story, such as Prince Edward Island, etc.

2.9 B.C. as abbreviation of Canadian province must be preceded by town name; B.C., the era, must be preceded by a date.

2.10 ABBREVIATE U.S.S.R. and U.A.R. in datelines.

2.11 ABBREVIATE United Nations and United States in titles: U.S. Junior Chamber of Commerce (Jaycees as exception in abbreviation by letters), U.N. Educational, Scientific and Cultural Organization (UNESCO). (See 2.1, 3.3)

151

2.12 Spell United States and United Nations when used as a noun. U.S.A. and U.N. as nouns may be used in texts or direct quotations.

2.13 ABBREVIATE and capitalize religious, fraternal, scholastic or honorary degrees, etc., but lower case when spelled: B.A., bachelor of arts. (See 8.4)

2.14 ABBREVIATE titles and capitalize: Mr., Mrs., M., Mlle., Dr., Prof., Sen., Rep., Asst., Lt. Gov., Gov. Gen., Supt., Atty. Gen., Dist. Atty., in titles before names but not after names. Do not abbreviate attorney in: The statement by defense attorney John Jones, etc. (See 1.7)

2.15 Mr. is used only with Mrs., or with clerical titles (except in texts or verbatim quotes). (See 8.4, 8.9, 8.10)

2.16 Do NOT abbreviate port, association, point, detective, department, deputy, commandant, commodore, field marshal, general manager, secretary-general, secretary, treasurer, fleet admiral or general of the armies (but Adm. Nimitz or Gen. Pershing is correct). (See 2.21)
Do NOT abbreviate "guaranteed annual wage" and do NOT abbreviate Christmas.

2.17 ABBREVIATE months when used with dates: Oct. 12, 1492; but spell out otherwise as October 1492. Abbreviations for months are Jan., Feb., Aug., Sept., Oct., Nov., Dec. Do not abbreviate March, April, May, June or July except in tabular or financial routine where the abbreviations are Mar, Apr, Jun, Jly and spell May.

2.18 Days of the week are abbreviated only in tabular matter or financial routine where they are Mon, Tue, Wed, Thu, Fri, Sat, Sun. The proper word division for Wednesday is: Wednes-day.

2.19 ABBREVIATE St. and Ste. as in Sault Ste. Marie, St. Louis, St. Lawrence, etc. (except Saint John, N.B.). Abbreviate the mountain but spell the city: Mt. Everest, Mount Vernon; Abbreviate army post but spell city: Ft. Sill, Fort Meyer.

2.20 Do not abbreviate Alexander, Benjamin, Charles, Frederick, William, etc., as Alec, Alex, Ben., Benj., Chas., etc., unless person does so himself. Follow person's preference.

152

2.21 Military abbreviations:

ARMY

General	Gen.
Lieutenant General	Lt. Gen.
Major General	Maj. Gen.
Brigadier General	Brig. Gen.
Colonel	Col.
Lieutenant Colonel	Lt. Col.
Major	Maj.
Captain	Capt.
Lieutenant	Lt.
Chief Warrant Officer	CWO
Warrant Officer	WO
Sergeant Major	Sgt. Maj.
Specialist Nine	Spec. 9
Master Sergeant	M. Sgt.
First Sergeant	1st. Sgt.
Specialist Eight	Spec. 8
Platoon Sergeant	Platoon Sgt.
Sergeant First Class	Sgt. 1.C.
Specialist Seven	Spec. 7
Staff Sergeant	S. Sgt.
Specialist Six	Spec. 6
Sergeant	Sgt.
Specialist Five	Spec. 5
Corporal	Cpl.
Specialist Four	Spec. 4
Private First Class	Pfc.
Private	Pvt.
Recruit	Rct.

NAVY, COAST GUARD

Admiral	Adm.
Vice Admiral	Vice Adm.
Rear Admiral	Rear Adm.
Commodore	Commodore
Captain	Capt.
Commander	Cmdr.
Lieutenant Commander	Lt. Cmdr.
Lieutenant	Lt.
Lieutenant Junior Grade	Lt. (j.g.)
Ensign	Ens.
Commissioned Warrant Officer	CWO
Warrant Officer	WO
Master Chief Petty Officer	M.CPO
Senior Chief Petty Officer	S.CPO
Chief Petty Officer	CPO

Petty Officer 1st Class	PO 1.C.
Petty Officer Second Class	PO 2.C.
Petty Officer Third Class	PO 3.C.
Seaman	Seaman
Seaman Apprentice	Seaman Appren.
Seaman Recruit	Seaman Rct.

MARINE CORPS

Commissioned officers are abbreviated the same as Army, warrant officers the same as Navy. Noncommissioned designations are the same as Army except specialist and:

Master Gunnery Sergeant	Mgy. Sgt.
Gunnery Sergeant	Gunnery Sgt.
Lance Corporal	Lance Cpl.

AIR FORCE

Air Force commissioned officers are abbreviated the same as Army. Noncommissioned designations include:

Chief Master Sergeant	CM. Sgt.
Senior Master Sergeant	SM. Sgt.
Master Sergeant	M. Sgt.
Technical Sergeant	T. Sgt.
Staff Sergeant	S. Sgt.
Airman 1st Class	Airman 1.C.
Airman 2nd Class	Airman 2.C.
Airman 3rd Class	Airman 3.C.
Airman Basic	Airman

The Air Force also may designate certain other descriptions as radarman, navigator, etc., but such designations are not abbreviated.

The Navy has numerous ratings such as machinist, torpedoman, etc., and they are not abbreviated.

The Army, Coast Guard and Marine Corps also may describe personnel by specific duty in addition to rank.

Note: The period is used in several abbreviations, such as Spec. 1.C., in Teletypesetter in the absence of the diagonal or slash mark.

Punctuation III

Punctuation in printing serves the same purpose as voice inflection in speaking. Proper phrasing avoids ambiguity, insures clarity and lessens need for punctuation.

THE PERIOD

3.1 The period is used after a declarative or imperative sentence: The facing is Vermont marble. Shut the door.

The period is used after a question intended as a suggestion: Tell how it was done.

The period is used in summary form:

1. Korean War. 2. Domestic policy. A. Punctuate properly. B. Write simply.

3.2 The period is used for ellipsis and in some columnist material. Ellipsis: The combine . . . was secure.

Column: Esther Williams gets the role. . . . John Hay signed a new contract. Rephrasing to avoid ellipses is preferable.

3.3 The period is used in abbreviations: U.S., U.N., c.o.d., etc. (See Section II for variations)

3.4 The period separates integer and decimal: 3.75 per cent; $8.25; 1.25 meters. (See 7.1, 7.2, 7.5, 7.7)

3.5 The period is omitted after a letter casually used as a name, and where a person omits the period in his name:

A said to B that he was not watching.

Herman B Wells (his usage). (See 1.33)

THE COMMA

3.6 The comma separates words or figures:

What the solution is, is a question.

Aug. 1, 1960.   1,234,567

The comma serves in a series:

The woman was short, slender, blonde, well-dressed and old.

x, y and z.   1, 2 and 3.

The Selma, Ala., group saw the governor.

3.7 Do not use comma before "of": Brown of Arkadelphia.

3.8 Newspaper usage has, in most cases, eliminated the comma before "and" and "or" but this practice does not lessen the need for the mark in:
Fish abounded in the lake, and the shore was lined with deer.

3.9 The comma is used to set off attribution: The work, he said, is exacting. It is used in scores: Milwaukee 6, St. Louis 5.

3.10 The comma is used to separate in apposition or contrast:
Smithwick, the favorite, won handily.
But: The car that failed had been ahead.

3.11 The comma is omitted before Roman numerals, Jr., Sr., the ampersand, dash, in street addresses, telephone numbers and serial numbers:
Louis XVI, John Jones Jr., Smith & Co., ORegon 3-3617, 12345 Oak St., A1234567. (See 4.4)

THE SEMICOLON

3.12 The semicolon separates phrases containing commas to avoid confusion, and separates statements of contrast and statements too closely related:
The draperies, which were ornate, displeased me; the walls, light blue, were pleasing.
The party consisted of B. M. Jordan; R. J. Kelly, his secretary; Mrs. Jordan; Martha Brown, her nurse; and three servants. (Without the semicolons, that could be read as nine persons.)

THE APOSTROPHE

3.13 The apostrophe indicates the possessive case of nouns, omission of figures, and contractions.
Usually the possessive of a singular noun not ending in "s" is formed by adding the apostrophe and "s"; the plural noun by adding the "s" and then the apostrophe: boys' wear, men's wear.
The apostrophe also is used in the plural possessive "es"; Joneses' house.
The "s" is dropped and only the apostrophe used in "for conscience' sake" or in a sibilant double or triple "s" as "Moses' tablet."
In single letters: A's.

3.14 The apostrophe is used in contractions: I've, isn't; in omission of figures: '90, '90s, class of '22. (See 4.3)

3.15 The apostrophe use or lack of should follow the official name of group, institution, locality, etc.: Johns Hopkins University, Actors Equity Association, Court of St. James's (variation of possessive ending).

THE COLON

3.16 The colon precedes the final clause summarizing prior matter; introduces listings, statements and texts; marks discontinuity, and takes the place of an implied "for instance":
The question came up: What does he want to do? (See 1.31)
States and funds allotted were: Alabama $6,000; Arizona $4,000, etc.

3.17 The colon is used in clock time: 8:15 p.m. (See 4.9)

3.18 The colon is used in Bible and legal citations:
Matt 2:14. Missouri Statutes 3: 245-260.

THE EXCLAMATION POINT

3.19 The exclamation point is used to indicate surprise, appeal, incredulity or other strong emotion:
How wonderful!   What!   He yelled, "Come here!"

THE QUESTION MARK

3.20 The question mark follows a direct question, marks a gap or uncertainty and in the latter use is enclosed in parentheses:
What happened to Jones?
It was April 13 (?) that I saw him.
The mark also is used in public proceedings, interviews, etc.:
Q. Were you there? A. I don't recall.
Exception: Where, in interviews, the question or answer is of some length, it is preferable to paragraph both Q. and A.

PARENTHESES

3.21 Parentheses set off material, or an element of a sentence.
It is not the custom (at least in the areas mentioned) to stand at attention.

3.22 Where location identification is needed but is not part of the official name: The Springfield (Ohio) Historical Society edition, etc. It is not necessary to bracket: The Springfield, Ohio, area population, etc.

3.23 Parentheses are not used around political-geographical designation: Sen. Theodore Francis Green, D-R.I., and Rep. Charles A. Halleck, R-Ind., were invited. (See 2.6)

3.24 Parentheses set off letters or figures in a series: The order of importance will be (a) general acceptance, (b) costs, and (c) opposition.

3.25 Where part of a sentence is parenthetical and the punctuation mark comes at the end of the sentence it goes outside:
He habitually uses two words incorrectly (practical and practicable).
Ordinarily the mark goes inside: (The foregoing was taken from an essay.)
Several paragraphs of parenthetical matter start with the opening mark on each paragraph and the final paragraph is ended with a closing parenthesis with the punctuation inside.

QUOTATION MARKS

3.26 Quotation marks enclose direct quotations; are used around phrases in ironical uses; around slang expressions; misnomers; titles of books, plays, poems, songs, lectures or speeches when the full title is used; hymns; movies; TV programs, etc. (See 1.30, 10.14)

3.27 Use quotation marks instead of parentheses around nicknames apart from the name: Smith, who weighed 280, was called "Slim."
Harold "Red" Grange.
The comma and period are placed inside the quotation marks. Other punctuation is placed according to construction:
Why call it a "gentlemen's agreement"?
The sequence in multiple quotations:
"The question is 'Does his position violate the "gentlemen's 'post-haste' agreement" so eloquently described by my colleague as "tommyrot"?' "

THE DASH

3.28 The dash indicates a sudden change. Examples:
He claimed—no one denied it—that he had priority.
It can be used instead of parentheses in many cases: 10 pounds—$28—paid.
If that man should gain control—God forbid!—our troubles will have only begun.
The monarch—shall we call him a knave or a fool?—approved it.

3.29 The dash is used after the logotype and before the first word of a story:
NEW YORK (logotype)—Mayor, etc.

3.30 The dash also is used as the minus sign in temperatures to indicate below-zero temperature: Duluth −12.

THE HYPHEN

3.31 The hyphen is one of the least correctly used, and most abused, marks. It is used properly to form compound words, to divide words in composition, in figures, in some abbreviations, and to separate double vowels in some cases.

The general rule for hyphens is that "like" characters take the hyphen, "unlike" characters do not.

A-bomb, U-boat, 20-20 vision, 3D, B60, MIG17, 3-2 (odds and scores), secretary-treasurer, south-southwest, north-central.

Exception: 4-H Club.

3.32 Adjectival use must be clear. (See 5.6)

The 6-foot man eating shark was killed (the man was).

The 6-foot man-eating shark was killed (the shark was).

3.33 Suspensive hyphenation:

The A- and H-bombs were exploded.

The 5- and 6-year-olds attend morning classes.

3.34 Ordinarily in prefixes ending in vowels and followed by the same vowel, the hyphen is used: pre-empt, re-elect. (Check dictionary for exceptions such as cooperate, coed, coordinates, etc.)

3.35 NEVER use the hyphen with adverb ending in "ly" such as badly damaged, fully informed, newly chosen, etc.

3.36 The hyphen also serves to distinguish meaning of similarly spelled words: recover, re-cover; resent, re-sent.

3.37 The hyphen also separates a prefix from a proper noun: pre-Raphaelite, un-American, etc.

3.38 The prefix "ex" is hyphened: ex-champion.

3.39 The hyphen has been abandoned in newspaper usage in weekend, worldwide, nationwide, etc.

THE AMPERSAND

3.40 The ampersand is used in abbreviations and firm names: Jones & Co., AT&T, etc. (See 2.3)

Numerals IV

In general, spell below 10, use numerals for 10 and above.

4.1 Numerals are used exclusively in tabular and statistical matter, records, election returns, times, speeds, latitude and longitude, temperatures, highways, distances, dimensions, heights, ages, ratios, proportions, military units, political divisions, orchestra instruments, court districts or divisions, handicaps, betting odds and dates (Fourth of July and July Fourth acceptable).

Use figures in all man or animal ages. Spell under 10 for inanimates: four-mile-trip, four miles from the center, etc.

Exceptions Fifth Avenue, Fifth Republic of France (See 1.25, 2.4), Big Ten, Dartmouth eleven.

The forms: 3-year-old girl, the girl is 3, 5 feet 2, 5-foot-2 trench, Washington won, 6-3; $10 shirt, seven-cent stamp, eight-hour day, five-day week, 60 cents (See 4.6), .38-caliber pistol.

6:30 p.m. or 6:30 o'clock Monday night (never 6:30 p.m. Monday night, or 6:30 p.m. o'clock). (See 6.15)

The vote was 1,345 for and 1,300 against.

The ratio was 6 to 4, but the 6-4 ratio.

It is 20th century but Twentieth Century Limited (train).

In series, keep the simplest related forms:

There are 3 ten-room houses, 1 fourteen-room house, 25 five-room houses and 40 four-room houses in the development.

$4 million but four million persons—the $ is equivalent of second numeral.

4.2 Numerals: 6th Fleet, 1st Army, 2nd Division, 10th Ward, 22nd District, 8th U.S. Circuit Court of Appeals.

Arabic numerals for spacecraft, missiles, etc.

4.3 Casual numbers are spelled:

A thousand times no! Gay Nineties. (See 3.14)

Wouldn't touch it with a ten-foot pole (but: The flag hung from a 10-foot pole—an exact measure).

4.4 Roman numerals are used for personal sequence, Pope, war, royalty, act, yacht and horse: John Jones III (some may prefer and use 3rd), Pope John XXIII, World War I, King George V, Act II, Shamrock IX, Hanover II. (See 3.11)

4.5 Highways: U.S. 301, Interstate 90, Illinois 34.

4.6 In amounts of more than a million, round numbers take the dollar sign and million, billion, etc., are spelled. Decimalization is carried to two places: $4.35 million.

Exact amounts would be: $4,351,242.

Less than a million the form: $500, $1,000, $650,000, etc.

The same decimalization form is used for figures other than money such as population, automobile registration, etc. (See 4.1)

Spell "cents" in amounts less than a dollar. (See 4.1, 7.5)

See Section VII for exceptions in market routine.

In ranges: $12 million to $14 million (or billion) not $12 to $14 million (or billion).

4.7 The English pound sign is not used. Spell "pounds" after figures and convert to dollars. (See 3.28)

4.8 Fractions in Teletypesetter are confined to matrices of 8ths: ⅛, ¼, ⅜, ½, ⅝, ¾, ⅞. Other fractions require the hyphen 3-16, 9-10, 1-3, etc.

Fractions used alone are spelled: three-fourths of a mile.

If the diagonal or slash (/) is incorporated in Teletypesetter operation, that symbol will replace the hyphen in fractions other than 8ths. The "plus" sign now occupies that casting-machine channel in the agate font and the hyphen will continue to be used in the agate font for fractions other than 8ths.

Stories dealing with percentages use figures; an isolated one-time reference under 10 is spelled as: four per cent of the population is illiterate.

4.9 Time sequences are given in figures: 2:30:21.6 (hours, minutes, seconds, tenths). (See 3.17)

4.10 Metric measurements use the comma in three-figure sequences except that kilocycles and meters in electronics are printed solid unless 10ths are included and the 10ths are set off by a period.

4.11 Serial numbers are printed solid: A1234567.

4.12 Write it No. 1 boy. No. 2 candidate, etc.

Spelling V

The first preference in spelling is the short version in Webster's New International Dictionary with exceptions as given in this section; the U.S. Postal Guide; The U.S. Board of Geographic Names and National

Geographic Society with exceptions as given in this section. The news services have agreed on some spellings where authorities do not agree.

5.1 The following list includes agreed spellings:

Algiers	Cologne	Kingstown	Romania
Antioch	Copenhagen	Kurile	Rome
Antwerp	Corfu	Leghorn	Saint John, N.B.
Archangel	Corinth	Lisbon	St. John's, Nfld.
Athens	Dunkerque	Macao	Salonika
Baghdad	Florence	Madagascar	Sofia
Bangkok	Formosa Strait	Marseille	Taipei
Basel	Frankfurt	Mt. Sinai	Tehran
Bayreuth	Genoa	Mukden	Thailand
Beirut	Goteberg	Munich	Tiflis
Belgrade	Gulf of Riga	Naples	Turin
Bern	The Hague	North Cape	Valetta
Brunswick	Hamelin	Nuernberg	Mt. Vesuvius
Bucharest	Hannover	Peking	Vietnam
Cameroon	Hong Kong	Pescadores I.	Warsaw
Cape Town	Jakarta	Prague	Wiesbaden
Coblenz	Katmandu	Rhodes	Zuider Zee

5.2 Where old and new names are used, or where quoted material uses a different form, one is bracketed: Formosa (Taiwan) ; Gdansk (Danzig), etc.

5.3 In Chinese names, the name after the hyphen is lower case: Chiang Kai-shek, Mao Tse-tung.
It is Peking People's Daily, People's Republic, etc.

5.4 Often used and frequently misspelled: (*preferred spelling)

adviser	consul	hitchhiker	restaurant
accommodate	copilot	homemade	rock 'n' roll
anyone	copter	home town	schoolteacher
Asian flu	council	impostor	sit-down
ax	counsel	ionosphere	skillful
baby-sit	disc	isotope	strait jacket
baby sitter	drought	judgment	strong-arm
baby-sitting	drunken	jukebox	subpoena
baritone	employe*	kidnaping	swastika
blond, male	embarrass	likable	teen-age
blonde, female, hue	eyewitness	machine gun	under way
box office	fallout	missile	vacuum
box-office sales	fire fighter	naphtha	wash 'n' wear
cannot	fulfill	old-timer	weird
cave-in	goodby*	per cent	wheel chair
chauffeur	good will, noun	percentage	whisky
cigarette	goodwill, adj.	permissible	wiretapping
clue	hanged	post office	X ray, noun
consensus	harass	propeller	X-ray, adj.

Disc is a phonograph record, National Council of Disc Jockeys is the trade organization.

It is drunken driving.

Be sure of words ending in ise, ize, and yse.
It is GI and GIs for persons, GI's and GIs' for possessive.

A consonant after a vowel and ending in a final accented syllable is doubled: corral, corralled; transfer, transferred; canal, canalled.

A consonant is not doubled when the accent falls on an earlier syllable: total, totaled; kidnap, kidnaped; channel, channeled; cancel, canceled.
It is bus and buses—buss is not a vehicle.

5.5 In compounding, meaning should be the guide. A great grandfather means he is great; a great-grandfather is lineage. Three-piece suits at $100 a piece would be $300 each; three-piece suits at $100 apiece would be $100 each.

It is right-hander, right-handed, left-wing group, left-winger but the left wing of the party.

5.6 "Air" is solid in airplane, airline, airport, airwave, airship, etc. Some corporate names divide airline: Eastern Air Lines (EAL), United Air Lines (UAL).

5.7 Some of the general rules for prefixes and suffixes:
all (prefix) hyphenated: All-Star.
ante, anti (prefix) solid: antebellum, antiaircraft—except in proper noun usage which is anti-American, etc.
bi (prefix) solid: biennial, bifocal.
co (prefix) usually solid: copilot, coed, etc.
counter (prefix) solid; counterfoil, etc.
down (prefix and suffix) solid: downstroke, touchdown.
electro (prefix) solid: electrolysis.
ex (prefix) hyphenated: ex-champion.

extra (prefix) solid: extraterritorial.
fold (suffix) solid: twofold
goer (suffix) solid: churchgoer.
in (prefix): insufferable; (suffix) hyphenated: stand-in
infra (prefix) solid: infrared.
inter (prefix) solid: interstate.
intra (prefix) solid: intrastate, intramural.
multi (prefix) solid: multimillion, multifaced.
non (prefix) solid: nonpartisan, nonsupport.
out (prefix) hyphenated: out-talk, out-box.
over (prefix and suffix) solid: overcome, pushover.
post (prefix) solid: postwar (but it is post-mortem).
pre (prefix) solid: predetermined, predawn.
self (prefix) hyphenated: self-defense.
semi (prefix) solid: semiannual.

sub (prefix) solid: subzero.
super (prefix) solid: superabundance, superman.
trans (prefix) solid: transatlantic, transcontinental (but trans-Canada with proper noun of country).
tri (prefix) solid: trifocal.
ultra (prefix) solid: ultraviolet.

un (prefix) solid: unshaven, unnecessary (but un-American with proper noun).
under (prefix) solid: underground, underdog, undersold.
uni (prefix) solid: unicolor.
wide (suffix) solid: worldwide, nationwide.

Miscellaneous VI

6.1 Engine is correct, not motor, in aviation; twin-engine, six-engine, etc. Exception: Trimotor, an obsolete plane but it still occurs in news stories. In railroading, power plants are locomotives—electric, steam, diesel. Diesels also may be called units, or engines.

6.2 Jet planes are driven solely by turbine engines. If the jet engine turns a propeller, it is a turboprop. True jets include the Boeing 707, Douglas DC8, Convair 880, de Havilland Comet, French Caravelle and numerous military (naval) planes. Turboprops include Lockheed Electra, Fairchild F27, Bristol Britannia, Vickers Viscount.

Propeller-driven planes include Super Constellation C, Douglas DC6B, Boeing Stratocruiser.

Flier is an aviator, flyer is a train.

6.3 A wife becomes a widow on the death of her husband. It is redundant to say "widow of the late." "John Jones is survived by his widow" (not wife).

6.4 Include in first reference the first name and initials, or names or initials according to preference of person: Sen. Theodore Francis Green, D. H. Lawrence. (See 1.33, 9.7)

Correct spelling: Randolph McC. Pate. Howard McC. Snyder.

6.5 Long titles: (See 1.6)
International Brotherhood of Teamsters, Chauffeurs, Warehousemen and Helpers is shortened to Teamsters Union, and in subsequent references to Teamsters.

Cemetery Workers and Green Attendants Union of the Building Service Employes International Union is shortened to Cemetery Workers Union.

6.6 An automatic is not a revolver and vice versa, but "pistol" describes either. A bullet is the metal projectile of a cartridge which includes the propellant powder, casing and primer.

Shell describes military and naval or shotgun ammunition.

6.7 Weather: See Webster for Weather Bureau wind scale which has replaced the Beaufort wind scale.

Be certain in the use of tornado, cyclone, typhoon, monsoon, hurricane, etc. The U.S. Weather Bureau defines a blizzard:

"Generally when there are winds of 35 m.p.h., or more which whip falling snow, or snow already on the ground, and temperatures are 20 degrees above zero Fahrenheit, or lower.

"A severe blizzard is where winds are 45 m.p.h. or more, temperatures 10 degrees above zero or lower, and great density of snow either falling or whipped from the ground."

Neither is a hard and fast rule, the bureau says, because winds and temperatures may vary but blizzard-like conditions may prevail.

Rule of thumb: Do not call a snowstorm a blizzard unless the Weather Bureau describes it as such.

In weather stories, with addition of Alaska and Hawaii as states, it is incorrect to refer to highest or lowest temperatures "in the nation" if figures from those two states are not included. The Weather Bureau has a phrase to cover the omission: It refers to minimums and maximums in the "48 contiguous states."

6.8 There are policemen, detectives, deputies, investigators, etc., but not "lawmen."

6.9 Avoid making verbs out of nouns: shotgunned to death, suicided, etc.

Avoid trite phrases of dialect, especially "Sure and it was" and "begorra" etc., in March 17 stories.

If a record is set it is new—"new record" is redundant.

6.10 In describing someone or something from Washington, make clear it is the state or District of Columbia.

6.11 Fahrenheit is used most frequently to measure degrees of heat and cold. If centigrade occurs in foreign, or scientific, copy conversion to Fahrenheit is nine-fifths times centigrade plus 32.

The Kelvin scale of temperature will come into use oftener. Temperatures are referred to in this scale as "degrees absolute" or "degrees Kelvin." Absolute zero in the Kelvin scale is 460 degrees below Fahrenheit zero; 273 degrees below centigrade zero.

6.12 A knot is a unit of speed and is equivalent to 6,076.10 feet an hour. The knot is a nautical mile computed as the length of one minute of the meridian. To convert knots into approximate statute miles per hour, multiply knots by 1.15. It is incorrect to say "sailed 14 knots an hour."

6.13 Gross tonnage is a necessary part of any story dealing with commercial shipping as the accepted basic measurement of size. Naval vessels list "displacement tonnage."

6.14 Red-headed means a red head; red-haired means hair of that color. A person may be called a "redhead" jocularly but is not properly described as "red-headed."

6.15 It is not necessary to bracket time zones in ordinary happenings such as accidents, shootings, etc. It is sufficient to say something occurred at 11 p.m. (See 4.1)

Zone should be included in earthquakes, radio and TV broadcast times. Convert to EST.

Informative notes to editors giving times should include the zone.

6.16 G, G-force, is gravitational pull equal to about 32 feet per second, a second, in acceleration. Thus a flier (plane, rocket, etc.) subjected to a force of 5 G's is accelerating at five times the force of gravity at the earth's surface, or roughly at a 160-foot-a-second, per-second, rate.

6.17 Mach numbers refer to the

speed of a body (aircraft, missile, etc.) in relation to the speed of sound. Mach 2 would be twice the speed of sound. A rule of thumb for speed of sound is 750 miles an hour at sea level, and 660 miles an hour at 30,000 feet.

6.18 Thrust is the measure of a driving force, or power, expressed in pounds. Jet engine and rocket powers are expressed in pounds. Thrust in pounds times speed in miles per hour divided by 375 converts thrust to horsepower.

Appendix II

Glossary of Terms

Many newspaper terms are not used in radio and television. However, there are some terms that apply to print and broadcast journalism. The terms in capital letters in the newspaper glossary below apply to both.

Newspaper Glossary

Ad: An advertisement.

ADD: Additions to a news story.

ADVANCE: A news story about a future event.

AMs: Morning newspapers.

ANGLE: An approach to a story or portion of a story.

ANPA: American Newspaper Publishers Association.

AP: Associated Press.

APME: Associated Press Managing Editors.

Art: An illustration for the newspaper. (Sometimes used in television.)

ASSIGNMENT: Duty given to a journalist.

Banner: A headline that extends across the entire page, sometimes called a **streamer** or **line**.

BEAT: Those places visited regularly by a reporter; also an exclusive news story.

BODY: Portion of news story that follows the lead.

BOOK: Packet of copy paper and carbons on which news stories are written.

BOIL: To condense or compress a news story.

Box: A news story enclosed in rules.

Bulldog: Early newspaper edition.

BULLETIN: An urgent wire service story.

Byline: The writer's name at the top of a news story.

CAPS: Capital letters.

Caption: Descriptive material that accompanies a piece of art (photograph, map, any illustration).

City room: Newspaper newsroom.

COPY: Material written by a journalist.

COPY EDITORS: Those persons who edit news copy. In newspaper newsrooms they are sometimes called copyreaders.

CORRESPONDENT: An out-of-town reporter, sometimes a part-time reporter.

COVER: To obtain news.

CREDIT LINE: A line that designates the source of a picture, cartoon, illustration, film story.

Crop: Reducing the size of an illustration before it is put into printed form.

Cutlines: The part of a caption, usually set in bold-face type, that describes a picture, cartoon or illustration.

DATELINE: The place at which an event happened, usually placed at the beginning of a newspaper story.

DEADLINE: Closing time for all news copy for a particular newspaper edition or broadcast news program.

DESKMAN: A news editor in the newsroom.

DOPE STORY: Also called a "think piece."

DUPE: A carbon copy of a news story.

Ears: The upper corners of the front page.

Edition: Newspapers containing the same matter; printed during one press run.

EDITORIAL: Comment on news; opinion expressed by the news organization.

FILLER: Small items used to fill out columns where needed; fill material in a radio or television news program.

FEATURE: A news story of human interest that is not hard or spot news; usually anything of a non-news nature.

Flag: The title or name of the newspaper at the top of the front page.

Folio: The number of each newspaper page.

FLASH: In hard news, a word used infrequently to describe the first report of a momentous event.

Galley: A metal tray used to hold type after it has been set.

FUTURE BOOK: Date book of future events; sometimes called futures file.

Gang coverage: Mass coverage of a major news event by one news organization.

HANDOUT: A publicity release.

Head: A headline.

HOLD FOR RELEASE: Instruction placed on a news story that must not be released until a certain day or time or notification.

HTK: Abbreviation of "Head To Kum" meaning headline to come; also the title of a book on headline writing by John B. Bremner.

HUMAN INTEREST: News feature stories with emotional appeal.

INSERT: Addition to a story written in such a way that it can be placed between two existing paragraphs.

Italics: Type face with characters slanted to the right.

Jump: That part of a front page story continued to an inside page.

Jump line: A line of type giving the succeeding, or preceding, page numbers of a story.

KILL: To eliminate news material at any stage of processing.

LEAD: Beginning of a story.

LEGMAN: A reporter who gathers but usually does not write news or does not broadcast news in the case of large broadcast news operations.

LIBEL: Any defamatory statement expressed in writing.

Lockup: Deadline in the composing room for getting all page forms into the stereotype department.

LOWER CASE: Small letters.

Makeup: Assembling the newspaper in the composing room.

Makeover: To change the arrangement of type and cuts in a page of type and cast a new stereotype plate of the page.

Masthead: The standing heading on the editorial page containing certain information about the newspaper.

MORGUE: News library.

Overhead: A news story sent by telegraph instead of by the leased wire.

OBIT: An announcement of a death; obituary.

OVERNIGHT: An assignment from the previous day; a story written the day before for use the following day.

Overset: Unused type left over from an edition.

Pickup: Direction to the printer to add to the relevant story certain matter that is already in type.

Pickup line: Line at the top of a newspaper wire service story that includes the word "add;" provides the last line of the previous material already transmitted.

PIX: Abbreviation for pictures.

PLAY: The display or treatment given to a story or picture or newsfilm story in the case of television.

PMs: Afternoon newspapers.

POOL: One or more newsmen or newswomen selected to cover an event for a large group of news reporters.

Proof: Inked impressions of type; used to make corrections.

QUERY: Message from correspondent, stringer, freelance writer or reporter offering a story for publication or broadcast.

RELEASE: The time stated by the news source for publication or broadcast of an advance news story.

Replate: To make over a page and stereotype it; makeover.

REWRITE MAN: A newspaper or wire service writer who writes or rewrites material from reporters outside the newsroom.

REVISE: (noun) A second proofsheet taken to check whether matter corrected on the original proofsheet was corrected as directed; (verb) to change a news story.

Rim: The outside edge of a horseshoe-shaped copy desk in the newsroom.

SCHEDULE: List of headlines or assignments for a particular edition or broadcast news program.

SCOOP: An exclusive news story.

SIDEBAR: A news story relating to a main news story that is an elaboration of the main story.

Slot: The inside space of a horseshoe-shaped copy desk where the head copyreader sits.

SHORT: A brief news story.

SLUG: An identifying name or slug usually put on a newspaper story by a copyreader or on a broadcast news story by the writer.

Split page: First page of a second section in a newspaper with two sections.

Stereotype: Plate cast from a mold of a page form of type.

Stet: Means "Let it stand." When written in the margin of a piece of copy it tells the printer to set the matter even though it has been marked out.

Stick: About two inches of type.

STRINGER: A part-time correspondent for a newspaper, wire service or broadcast news operation.

Take: The portion of a piece of copy to be set by the individual printer and later assembled with "takes" that other printers have set.

Time copy: News copy of a non-urgent nature usually set in advance and used as filler where needed.

THIRTY: Telegraphers' Morse Code symbol for "The End." Used by news writers to indicate the end of a story.

TIGHT: Word used to indicate there is not much news space available in the newspaper, or to indicate time is critical in a broadcast news program.

TRIM: To cut a news story.

Typo: A typographical error.

UPI: United Press International.

WIRE SERVICE: A press association.

WRAPUP: A news summary of events in a broadly developed news event or events.

Broadcast Glossary

A-roll: An edited reel of film used in a multiple-chain news story. An A-roll usually carries most of the picture to be used. (See B-roll).

Academy leader: Film containing numbers in reverse. It is used to guide the director and projectionist with a count down to the beginning of a film story.

Account: A reporter's version of a news story.

Aircheck: A recording made of a program as it was broadcast.

Airman: Anyone who performs on radio or television.

Airtime: The time when a news program is scheduled for broadcast.

Audio: Sound portion of a broadcast.

B-roll: Designation of a second edited reel of film when more than one film roll is used with one story. The B-roll usually carries silent film in multiple-chain presentations.

B & W: Black and white.

Back-timing: Timing of the last section of a news program.

Balance: Distribution of visual material in a television news program; geographic distribution of news; news content.

Barn door: Metal shades used to block light emission from a TV floodlamp.

Beeper: Telephone recording containing sound beeps at regular intervals.

Bloop: To erase the sound track on magnetic film with a small magnet.

Blurb: A publicity story in the form of a news or press release.

Boom: The pole or arm from which a mike hangs.

Budget: Amount of news copy needed to fill the allotted time of a news program.

Butt end: To splice one piece of film directly to another.

Break: The beginning of a story or the start of an important development in a running story.

Bridge: The sentence or phrase linking two news stories together.

Cast: Newscast or news program.

Closeup: A close shot.

Cold copy: News copy which the newsman has not had time to read before going on the air. Unfamiliar news copy.

Creepie peepie: A portable video camera.

CU: Closeup.

Cue: Hand signal giving directions or instructions.

Cue card: A card displaying a cue or instructions to the person on the air.

Cut: To delete material from a news script or to delete frames from a film clip; to end or suddenly stop. Used as a noun and verb.

Cutaway shot: Usually a film shot which takes action away from the master shot. Used to avoid a jump-cut.

Dead air: Silence during a program.

Dissolve: The smooth exchange from one picture to another.

Dolly: The movable platform for a film or video camera.

Double chain: Using two reels of film on two projectors simultaneously to present one story.

Double shot: Broadcasting two commercials back-to-back.

Double system: Separate sound and picture processes

used in shooting motion picture film; sound is synchronized to the film in the shooting process.

Dry: Lack of news.

Dub: Re-recording or copying film, video tape or audio tape; to make another copy.

Establishing shot: A camera shot which establishes the scene.

Fade: A transitional device used to fade out of film or a video picture to black or in from black.

FCC: Federal Communications Commission.

Film chain: Equipment that contains a motion picture projector, slide projector and a television camera; it converts film pictures and sound into electronic signals.

Format: The organization or desired grouping of elements within a specific program or segment of a radio or television news program.

Goof: An error or mistake occuring on the air.

ID: Station identification.

Jump cut: A cut, usually on film, in which the picture content suddenly changes position; an unreal change.

Kicker: Last item in a news program; usually a humorous or funny story. Sometimes called a zipper or stinger.

Lavalier mike: A microphone attached to a cord and suspended around a person's neck.

Leader: Blank film used between film stories or within film stories using two reels of film.

Lip flap: Movement of lips without sound.

Magazine: Film container which can be attached to the motion picture camera.

Montage: A film or video tape sequence not laid out in chronological order. Creates artistic effect.

Net: Network.

O & O: Owned and operated, network owned and operated stations.

Open mike: A "live" microphone; on the air.

Pan: Movement of a video or film camera across a scene or from one subject to another.

Playback: To repeat; play what has just been recorded.

Promo: Promotional announcement.

Prop: Property used on the news set such as chairs, desk, etc., television prop.

Raw stock: Unexposed film.

Rear Projection: A picture projected on a screen from the rear and viewed from the front of the screen.

RP: Rear projection.

Recap: To repeat a news story or stories.

Screen: To view video tape or film.

SIL: Silent film.

Slant: Treatment of a news story; point emphasized; approach taken.

SOF: Sound on film.

Spot: Commercial announcement.

Sustainer: Unsponsored program.

Stretch: To slow speech delivery; to slow the pace.

Super: Superimposure; white lettering on black cardboard photographed by a video camera and then combined electronically with another image; usually used to identify a person, place or thing.

Standupper: Film or video report, usually recorded at the scene of an event; sometimes aired live. Reporter stands facing the camera while presenting report.

Tag: An addition either to a news story or a commercial announcement.

TD: Television technical director.

Tip: Information on a news story; news tip.

Truck: To film while riding or walking.

Two shot: Video or film camera framing two persons.

Upcut: The loss of words at the beginning of film, video tape or live studio presentation.

UHF: Ultra high frequency; TV Channels 14 and above.

VHF: Very high frequency; TV Channels 2 through 13.

Vizmo: Television rear projection process.

VO: Voice over.

VTR: Video tape recording .

Woodshedding: To read aloud, to rehearse news copy before going on the air.

Zoom lens: A lens of variable focal length.

Appendix III

Canons of Journalism

The primary function of newspapers is to communicate to the human race what its members do, feel and think. Journalism, therefore, demands of its practitioners the widest range of intelligence, or knowledge, of experience, as well as natural and trained powers of observation and reasoning. To its opportunities as a chronicle are indissolubly linked its obligations as teacher and interpreter.

To the end of finding some means of codifying sound practices and just aspirations of American journalism, these canons are set forth:

I

Responsibility. The right of a newspaper to attract and hold readers is restricted by nothing but consideration of public welfare. The use of a newspaper makes the share of public attention it gains serve to determine its sense of responsibility, which it shares with every member of its staff. A journalist who uses his power for any selfish or otherwise unworthy purpose is faithless to a high trust.

II

Freedom of the Press. Freedom of the press is to be guarded as a vital right of mankind. It is the unquestionable right to discuss whatever is not explicitly forbidden by law, including the wisdom of any restrictive statue.

III

Independence. Freedom from all obligations except that of fidelity to the public interest is vital.

1. Promotion of any private interest contrary to the general welfare, for whatever reason, is not compatible with honest journalism. So-called news communications from private sources should not be published without public notice of their source or else substantiation of their claims to value as news, both in form and substance.

2. Partisanship, in editorial comment which knowingly departs from the truth, does violence to the best spirit of American journalism; in the news columns it is subversive of a fundamental principle of the profession.

IV

Sincerity, truthfulness, accuracy. Good faith with the reader is the foundation of all journalism worthy of the name.

1. By every consideration of good faith a newspaper is constrained to be truthful. It is not to be excused for lack of thoroughness or accuracy within its control, or failure to obtain command of these essential qualities.

2. Headlines should be fully warranted by the contents of the articles which they surmount.

V

Impartiality. Sound practice makes a clear distinction between news reports and expressions of opinion. News reports should be free from opinion or bias of any kind.

1. This rule does not apply to so-called special articles unmistakably devoted to advocacy or characterized by a signature authorizing the writer's own conclusions and interpretations.

VI

Fair play. A newspaper should not publish unofficial charges affecting reputation or moral character without an opportunity given to the accused to be heard; right practice demands the giving of such opportunity in all cases of serious accusation outside judicial proceedings.

1. A newspaper should not invade private rights or feelings without sure warrant of public right as distinguished from public curiosity.

2. It is the privilege, as it is the duty, of a newspaper to make prompt and complete correction of its own serious mistakes of fact or opinion, whatever their origin.

VII

Decency. A newspaper cannot escape conviction of insincerity if while professing high moral purposes, it supplies incentives to base conduct, such as are to be found in details of crime and vice, publication of which is not demonstrably for the general good. Lacking authority to enforce its canons, the journalism here represented can but express the hope that deliberate pandering to vicious instincts will encounter effective public disapproval or yield to the influence of a preponderant professional condemnation.

Appendix IV

Radio and TV News Directors Association Code of Ethics

(U.S. adopted code January 2, 1966
Canadian Association adopted code September, 1970)

The members of the Radio Television News Directors Association agree that their prime responsibility as newsmen—and that of the broadcasting industry as the collective sponsor of news broadcasting—is to provide to the public they serve a news service as accurate, full and prompt as human integrity and devotion can devise. To that end, they declare their acceptance of the standards of practice here set forth, and their solemn intent to honor them to the limits of their ability.

ARTICLE ONE

The primary purpose of broadcast newsmen—to inform the public of events of importance and appropriate interest in a manner that is accurate and comprehensive—shall override all other purposes.

ARTICLE TWO

Broadcast news presentations shall be designed not only to offer timely and accurate information, but also to present it in the light of relevant circumstances that give it meaning and perspective.

This standard means that news reports, when clarity demands it, will be laid against a pertinent factual background; that factors such as race, creed, nationality or prior status will be reported only when they are relevant; that comment or subjective content will be properly identified; and that errors in fact will be promptly acknowledged and corrected.

ARTICLE THREE

Broadcast newsmen shall seek to select material for a newscast solely on their evaluation of its merits as news.

This standard means that news will be selected on the criteria of significance, community and regional relevance, appropriate human interest and service to defined audiences. It excludes sensationalism or misleading emphasis in any form, and subservience to external or "interested" efforts to influence news selection and presentation, whether from within the broadcasting industry or from without. It requires that such terms as "bulletin" and "flash" be used only when the character of the news justifies them; that bombastic or misleading descriptions of newsroom facilities and personnel be rejected, along with undue use of sound and visual effects; and that promotional or publicity material be sharply scrutinized before use and identified by source or otherwise when broadcast.

ARTICLE FOUR

Broadcast newsmen shall at all times display humane respect for the dignity, privacy and the well-being of persons with whom the news deals.

ARTICLE FIVE

Broadcast newsmen shall govern their personal lives and such nonprofessional associations as may impinge on their professional activities in a manner that will protect them from conflict of interest, real or apparent.

ARTICLE SIX

Broadcast newsmen shall seek actively to present all news the knowledge of which will serve the public interest, no matter what selfish, uninformed or corrupt efforts attempt to color it, withhold it, or prevent its presentation. They shall make constant effort to open doors closed to the reporting of public proceedings with tools appropriate to broadcasting (including cameras and recorders), consistent with the public interest. They acknowledge the newsman's ethic of protection of confidential information and sources, and urge unswerving observation of it, except in instances in which it would clearly and unmistakably defy the public interest.

ARTICLE SEVEN

Broadcast newsmen recognize the responsibility borne by broadcasting for informed analysis, comment and editorial opinion on public events and issues. They accept the obligation of broadcasters, for the presentation of such matters by individuals whose competence, experience and judgment qualify them for it.

ARTICLE EIGHT

In court, broadcast newsmen shall conduct themselves with dignity, whether the court is in or out of session. They shall keep broadcast equipment as unobtrusive and silent as possible. Where court facilities are inadequate, pool broadcasts should be arranged.

ARTICLE NINE

In reporting matters that are or may be litigated, the newsman shall avoid practices which would tend to interfere with the right of an individual to a fair trial.

ARTICLE TEN

Broadcast newsmen shall actively censure and seek to prevent violations of these standards, and shall actively encourage their observance by all newsmen, whether of the Radio Television News Directors Association or not.

Appendix V

Criteria of a Good Newspaper

(Associated Press Managing Editors Association, 1962)

A good newspaper prints the important news and provides the information, comment and guidance that is most useful to its readers.

It reports fully and explains the meaning of local, national and international events which are of major significance in its own community. Its editorial comment provides an informed opinion on matters of vital concern to its readers.

By reflecting the total image of its own community in its news coverage and by providing wise counsel in its editorials, a good newspaper becomes a public conscience. It also must be lively, imaginative and original; it must have a sense of humor, and the power to arouse keen interest.

To implement these principles of good editing requires a skilled staff, an attractive format, adequate space for news and comment and a sound business foundation.

The staff must possess the professional pride and competence necessary to breathe life and meaning into the daily record of history. Good writing must be combined with an effective typographical display of copy and pictures to capture the full drama and excitement of the day's news. Good printing is essential.

News and comment of most immediate interest and importance to the local community shall have priority for the available space, which will depend on the size and resources of the newspaper.

To assure a financially strong and independent publication, and one that is competitive with other media, a good newspaper must maintain effective circulation, advertising and promotion departments.

Finally, a good newspaper should be guided in the publication of all material by a concern for truth, the hallmark of freedom, by a concern for human decency and human betterment and by a respect for the accepted standards of its own community. A good newspaper may judge its own performance—and be judged—by the criteria that follow:

INTEGRITY

The newspaper shall:

(1) Maintain vigorous standards of honesty and fair play in the selection and editing of its content as well as in all relations with news sources and the public.

(2) Deal dispassionately with controversial subjects and treat disputed issues with impartiality.

(3) Practice humility and tolerance in the face of honest conflicting opinions or disagreement.

(4) Provide a forum for the exchange of pertinent comment and criticism, especially if it is in conflict with the newspaper's editoral point of view.

(5) Label its own editorial views or expressions of opinion.

ACCURACY

The newspaper shall:

(1) Exert maximum effort to print the truth in all news situations.

(2) Strive for completeness and objectivity.

(3) Guard against carelessness, bias or distortion by either emphasis or omission.

(4) Correct promptly errors of fact for which the newspaper is responsible.

RESPONSIBILITY

The newspaper shall:

(1) Use mature and considered judgment in the public interest at all times.

(2) Select, edit and display news on the basis of its significance and its genuine usefulness to the public.

(3) Edit news affecting public morals with candor and good taste and avoid an imbalance of sensational, predominately negative or merely trivial news.

(4) Accent when possible a reasonable amount of news which illustrates the values of compassion, self-sacrifice, heroism, good citizenship and patriotism.

(5) Clearly define sources of news, and tell the reader when competent sources cannot be identified.

(6) Respect rights of privacy.

(7) Instruct its staff members to conduct themselves with dignity and decorum.

LEADERSHIP

The newspaper shall:

(1) Act with courage in serving the public.

(2) Stimulate and vigorously support public officials, private groups and individuals in crusades and campaigns to increase the good works and eliminate the bad in the community.

(3) Help to protect all rights and privileges guaranteed by law.

(4) Serve as a constructive critic of government at all levels, provide leadership for necessary reforms or innovations and expose any misfeasance in office or any misuse of public power.

(5) Oppose demagogues and other selfish and unwholesome interests regardless of their size or influence.

Appendix VI

Television News Code— National Association of Broadcasters

(Section V, Television Code,
National Association of Broadcasters,
(13th edition, 1968)

THE TREATMENT OF NEWS AND PUBLIC EVENTS BY TELEVISION

1. A television station's news schedule should be adequate and well balanced.

2. News reporting should be factual, fair and without bias.

3. A television broadcaster should exercise particular discrimination in the acceptance, placement and presentation of advertising in news programs so that such advertising should be clearly distinguishable from the news content.

4. At all times, pictorial and verbal material for both news and comment should conform to other sections of these standards, wherever such sections are reasonably applicable.

5. Good taste should prevail in the selection and handling of news: morbid, sensational or alarming details not essential to the factual report, especially in connection with stories of crime or sex, should be avoided. News should be telecast in such a manner as to avoid panic and unnecessary alarm.

6. Commentary and analysis should be clearly identified as such.

7. Pictorial material should be chosen with care and not presented in a misleading manner.

8. All news interview programs should be governed by accepted standards of ethical journalism, under which the

interviewer selects the questions to be asked. Where there is advance agreement materially restricting an important or newsworthy area of questioning, the interviewer will state on the program that such limitation has been agreed upon. Such disclosure should be made if the person being interviewed requires that questions be submitted in advance or if he participates in editing a recording of the interview prior to its use on the air.

9. A television broadcaster should exercise due care in his supervision of content, format and presentation of newscasts originated by his station and in his selection of newscasters, commentators and analysts.

Bibliography

American Bar Association, **Law and Courts in the News**. Chicago: American Bar Association, 1960.

Michael J. Arlen, **Living-Room War**. New York: Viking Press, 1969.

Associated Press, **Style Book**. New York: Associated Press, 1970.

Associated Press, **Radio-Television News Style Book**. New York: Associated Press, 1952, 1962 and 1973.

Phillip H. Ault and Edwin Emery, **Reporting the News**. New York: Dodd-Mead and Co., 1959.

Theodore M. Bernstein, **Watch Your Language**. New York: Simon and Schuster, 1965.

Edward Bliss Jr. and John M. Patterson, **Writing News for Broadcast**. New York: Columbia University Press, 1971.

Chilton R. Bush, Newswriting and Reporting Public Affairs. Philadelphia: Chilton, 1965.

John B. Bremner, **HTK**. Topeka: Palindrome Press, 1972.

William F. Brooks, **Radio News Writing**. New York: McGraw-Hill, 1948.

Matthew J. Bruccoli, editor, **Ernest Hemingway, Cub Reporter**. Pittsburgh Press, 1970.

185

CBS News, **Television News Reporting**. New York: McGraw-Hill, 1958.

Mitchell V. Charnley, **Reporting**. New York: Holt, Rinehart and Winston, 1966.

Mitchell V. Charnley, **News by Radio**. New York: Macmillan, 1948.

David A. Dary, **Radio News Handbook**. Blue Ridge Summit, Pa.: TAB Books, 1970.

David A. Dary, **Television News Handbook**. Blue Ridge Summit, Pa.: TAB Books, 1971.

Ernest Dimnet, **The Art of Thinking**. New York: Simon and Schuster, 1955.

Edwin Emery, **The Press and America**. Englewood Cliffs, N.J.: Prentice-Hall, 1962.

Irving Fang, **Television News**. New York: Hastings House, 1968.

Rudolf Flesch, **The Art of Plain Talk**. New York: Harper and Bros., 1962.

Rudolf Flesch, **The Art of Readable Writing**. New York: Harper and Bros., 1962.

Maury Green, **Television News: Anatomy and Process**. Belmont, Calif.: Wadsworth, 1969.

Ben Gross, **I Looked and I Listened**. New York: Random House, 1954.

Harry F. Harrington and Elmo S. Watson, **Modern Feature Writing**. Harpers, 1935.

Robert Hilliard, **Writing for Television and Radio**. New York: Hastings House, 1962.

John Hohenberg, **The Professional Journalist**. New York: Holt, Rinehart and Winston, 1969.

Grant Milnor Hyde, **Newspaper Reporting**. New York: Prentice-Hall, 1952.

Grant Milnor Hyde, **Newspaper Reporting and Correspondence**. New York: D. Appleton and Co., 1919.

International News Service, **INS Radio News Manual**. New York: International News Service, 1947.

Robert F. Karolevitz, **Newspapering in the Old West**. Seattle: Superior, 1965.

Alexander Kendrick, **Prime Time: The Life of Edward R. Murrow**. Boston: Little-Brown, 1969.

Lewis Jordan, editor, **The New York Times Style Book**. New York: McGraw-Hill, 1962.

James Melvin Lee, **History of American Journalism**. New York: Garden City, 1923.

Carl E. Lindstrom, **The Fading American Newspaper**. New York: Doubleday, 1960.

Curtis D. MacDougall, **Interpretative Reporting**. New York: Macmillan, 1963.

Grant S. McCellan, editor, **Censorship in the United States**. New York: H. W. Wilson Co., 1967.

Frank Luther Mott, **American Journalism**. New York: Macmillan, 1949.

Phil Newsom, **United Press Radio News Style Book**. New York: United Press, 1943.

Walter Rae, **Editing Small Newspapers**. New York: M. S. Mill Co., 1943.

William L. Rivers, Theodore Peterson and Jay W. Jensen, **The Mass Media and Modern Society**. San Francisco: Rinehart Press, 1971.

A. A. Schechter with Edward Anthony, **I Live On Air**. New York: Stokes, 1941.

Irving Settel, **A Pictorial History of Radio**. New York: Citadel, 1960.

Irving Settel, **A Pictorial History of Television**. New York: Grosset and Dunlap, 1969.

Eric Sevareid, **Sounds in the Night**. New York: Knopf, 1956.
Eric Sevareid, **In One Ear**. New York: Knopf, 1952.

Bob Siller, Ted White and Hal Terkel, **Television and Radio News**. New York: Macmillan, 1960.

Bob Siller, **Guide to Professional Radio and TV Newscasting**. Blue Ridge Summit, Pa.: TAB Books, 1972.

Sam J. Slate and Joe Cook, **It Sounds Impossible**. New York: Macmillan, 1963.

Lowell Thomas, **History As You Heard It**. New York: Doubleday, 1957.

United Press International, **Broadcasting Style Book**. New York: United Press International, 1959 and 1969 editions.

United Press International, **Style Book**. New York: United Press International, 1970.

Luther Weaver, **The Technique of Radio Writing**. New York: Prentice-Hall, 1948.

Paul W. White, **News On The Air**. New York: Harcourt-Brace, 1947.

William Allen White, **The Autobiography of William Allen White**. New York: MacMillan, 1946.

William Wood, **Electronic Journalism**. New York: Columbia University Press, 1967.

Index